Creativity, Theology, and Posttraumatic Growth

Creativity, Theology, and Posttraumatic Growth

The Sacred Impulse of Play
and Transformation out of Tragedy

DUSTIN S. RISSER

PICKWICK *Publications* · Eugene, Oregon

CREATIVITY, THEOLOGY, and POSTTRAUMATIC GROWTH
The Sacred Impulse of Play and Transformation out of Tragedy

Pickwick Publications
An Imprint of Wipf and Stock Publishers
199 W. 8th Ave., Suite 3
Eugene, OR 97401

www.wipfandstock.com

PAPERBACK ISBN: 978-1-6667-3841-4
HARDCOVER ISBN: 978-1-6667-9907-1
EBOOK ISBN: 978-1-6667-9908-8

Cataloguing-in-Publication data:

Names: Risser, Dustin S., author.

Title: Creativity, theology, and posttraumatic growth : the sacred impulse of play and transformation out of tragedy / Dustin S. Risser.

Description: Eugene, OR: Pickwick Publications, 2022. | Includes bibliographical references and index.

Identifiers: ISBN 978-1-6667-3841-4 (paperback). | ISBN 978-1-6667-9907-1 (hardcover). | ISBN 978-1-6667-9908-8 (ebook).

Subjects: LSCH: Pastoral theology | Post-traumatic growth. | Life change events—Psychological aspects.

Classification: BR115.A8 R57 2022 (print). | BR115 (ebook).

VERSION NUMBER 080922

I want to give my heartfelt thank you to Tim and Kathy Risser for supporting me in prayer throughout my doctoral program, and upholding faith in God's inner working through the years of this project. Thank you to the brothers Alejandro and Marco Ulloa, for the many conversations that contributed to creativity, inspiration, and a life of faith. Blessings and thanks to all of those who were praying, encouraging and offering your support as this was being written; especially the Risser families, the Heisey family, Pisey Sok LMFT, Dr. Nadine Sidhom and the many others who have impacted me during different stages of idea generation, writing, and editing this work. By your walking with the Spirit in faith, hope and love you have contributed to my ability to complete this task. This work simply does come to fruition without such a grace.

Contents

Figures

Acknowledgments

I MUST EXPRESS MY sincere gratitude to my entire dissertation panel at Fuller Theological Seminary's School of Psychology and Marriage & Family Therapy. This panel was a lineup of experts in the global field of integration of Psychology and Theology. I want to thank Dr. Cynthia Eriksson for both her wisdom and commitment to whole-person research and clinical work in the areas of trauma, culture, and spirituality. Thank you to Dr. Pamela Ebstyne King, a forerunner in thriving, flourishing, and the integration of theology and developmental psychology, for her continued insight, inspiration and words of life spoken. Finally, a special thank you to my former advisor Dr. Brad D. Strawn, an innovator in intersection of Christian anthropology, psychoanalytic practice, and spiritual formation for your persistent encouragement, patience, and scholarly wisdom. I feel blessed to have had such an accomplished panel of experts in the field who brought both guidance, and genuine faith-filled reflection.

1

Introduction

THE HUMAN CAPACITY FOR creative play is widely regarded as a universal, intrinsic, and prehistoric human phenomenon (Morris-Kay, 2010). Creativity has been written into humanity's marrow, and people have witnessed its power in a host of forums. Such forums include traditional manifestations—such as music, dance, fine arts, design, cinema, and architecture; as well as practical and civic forums, such as collaborative economics, engineering, social policy, and scientific exploration. But perhaps the most essential forums have been the places where the very potential for creativity begins—the street corners, backyards, and family rooms across the globe.

Creativity has been a resource with nearly unlimited manifestations woven into the materialization of culture. Winnicott (1971) described such cultural materialization as emerging from a collective capacity for play, emphasizing the relational nature of creativity. Creativity has also been considered a core, developmental element of human flourishing (Russ, 2014). It is connected by emotional expression, bodily learning, and exploration, which come together in moments of spontaneity, initially in childhood. The power of curious spontaneity in childhood from which play emerges, may even be a developmental crux that can prepare creative resourcefulness later in life (Russ, 2014; Winnicott, 1965).

The unfolding of creative learning can be an opportunity for personal expression and emotional release, which might eventually unfold as personal growth and expansion of self-understanding throughout the lifespan (Garland et al., 2007; Hass-Cohen & Findlay, 2015; Winnicott, 1971). Given the varying roles of creativity in psychological development, emotional expression, and meaningful work, it is essential for Christian therapists to steward a theological understanding of creativity. From a perspective of Christian faith, the formative human potential of creativity is grounded in being created in the image of God (Gen 1:27). Creativity can be a gift that manifests the beauty, benevolence, patience, intrigue, and power of God, who is the Creator and origin of life-giving creativity (Moltmann et al., 1972).

Such a divinely originated capacity for creative living may also be a critical natural resource to humanity. The resource of creativity may help individuals integrate emotion, meaning, memory, bodily sensations, and complex learning together, in a synergistic experience that could facilitate recovery from psychological distress, and even result in personal growth. Clinically, creative activities have provided a therapeutic effect by helping individuals work through painful experiences, including those experiences as corrosive as trauma (Hass-Cohen, 2008; Russ, 2014). Though researchers have cited the use of art-making and creativity to improve psychological well-being, and benefit trauma recovery, few have focused on the role of art-making and creativity from a growth-oriented perspective (Crenshaw, 2006; Garland et al., 2007; Van der Kolk, 2014). Adding a dimension of growth within treatment could move clinicians beyond a perspective of solely recalibrating a person's distress level, and restoring their ability to function after trauma, to actually incorporating the possibility of worldview transformation, which may yield deep elements of self-discovery within the process (Janoff-Bulman, 2006; Kauffman & Gregoire, 2015).

The concept of psychological growth beyond the adverse effects of trauma, also known as posttraumatic growth (PTG; Calhoun & Tedeschi, 1998), has lacked clinical application to creative processes in current research. Art therapy has a recognized place in trauma treatment (Avrhami, 2006; Johnson et al., 2009), and has even demonstrated significant efficacy as an adjunctive treatment alongside Cognitive Processing Therapy (CPT), over and above CPT alone, for combat veterans with posttraumatic stress disorder (PTSD; Campbell et al., 2016). Yet using art-making as a route to capitalize on growth, beyond trauma, has been largely unrecognized. Though a few researchers have suggested creativity as a route to PTG (Chilton, 2013; Kaufman & Gregoire, 2015; Lee, 2013), it has lacked significant theoretical and systematic investigation. Particularly the hypothesis that creativity may contribute towards PTG, has lacked theoretical support; support which may have strong links to psychodynamic theory, especially concerning the underlying mechanisms of change in PTG. Additionally, there is rich history of theological themes of hope, transformation and redemption after traumatic experience in the Christian faith which can connect PTG with important theological themes, and dually towards the integration of faith and psychology.

But in order to thoughtfully understand PTG in context of other theories, PTG as a construct must be situated within a coherent wider-arching approach to trauma, as offered by Judith Herman (1997). Herman emphasized that the varieties of recovery from trauma occur in an undulating, nonlinear, and "dialectical" processes, which has included three central stages. Herman's (1997) stages included the "establishment of safety . . . remembrance and mourning . . . [and] reconnection with ordinary life" (p. 155). Researchers have described PTG as a theoretically undulating and dialectical construct (Calhoun & Tedeschi, 2013). Clinically, applying the creative process in the midst of trauma to promote growth would be primarily located in Herman's stages of remembrance and reconnection, as a traumatized person ought to have a baseline of psycho-physiologically informed coping and safety, before delving into more expressive creativity. But the limits of the construct and application of PTG should not deter clinicians from recognizing the potential such creative, positive movement has offered. Instead, the hope that can be gleaned from the process of recovery and growth might edify both Christian clinicians' and clients' vision of the presence of God's grace in creation, and the in-breaking of the Holy Spirit into the therapeutic process, even in the midst of dire traumatic narratives.

THESIS

Throughout this work, I provide psychological and theological grounds for the application of creativity as an adjunctive and ongoing therapeutic support, which might mobilize the occurrence of PTG. How might creative processes aid PTG from an embodied viewpoint? How can Christian theology support, inform, and empower the creative process? Further, how might such an experience of growth through the recovery of play impact an individual's sense of self, meaning-making system, and spirituality? In this work, I propose that experiences of creativity and play can offer a holistic approach to growth and transformation, after tragic and disorganizing experiences of trauma. This is accomplished by highlighting the interrelationship between creativity, Christian theology, and trauma in order to offer an integrated vision for promoting PTG.

METHOD

In the proceeding chapters I offer a psychological and theological account for the role of creativity, which has been applied to the construct of PTG. The role of creativity and play in psychological development (Russ, 1993; Russ, 2004; Russ, 2014) has remained a potent resource that can be harnessed toward PTG and solidified within the psychoanalytic theory of Winnicott. Winnicott's work can be applied broadly to the fundamental experience of play in shaping the self and interacting with the world in cogent ways. In addition, this work contributes to a theological understanding of creativity that provides an integrative frame for the Christian therapist. This highlights the role of experiences of liberation and wonder through creativity and play, as well as in Christian theology and spirituality. Liberation and wonder experienced through play anchor a perspective of renewal and growth for clients, in terms of both immediate and eschatological hope. With a psychologically and theologically informed perspective on the creative process, the application of this process towards PTG is then detailed. PTG is a relatively new concept of measurement in the field of psychology and reflects growth that occurs in various domains of life after a traumatic experience. This measurement was not meant to minimize the caustic effects of trauma, but was rather meant to track emergence that has occurred from worldview shifts. Instances of PTG, over time, have reoriented a hopeful attention to movement out of tragedy. PTG is the possible positive shift that can occur by a disturbance in worldview—which, when deconstructed, can open up a more robust posture of subjective experience and understanding oneself, others, and the environment. An experience of PTG, is not a given aspect of recovery, but is a possible change in the lens through which emboldened, richer colors may be illuminated in everyday life (Tedeschi & Calhoun, 1995; Tedeschi et al., 2018). The application of creativity towards PTG has offered a chance to extend growth and transformation beyond the therapy room by heightening agency; allowing for a holding space between sessions; increasing deliberative forms of rumination; adding depth and dimensionality to the post-trauma narrative; as well as offering a new mode of sharing a traumatic experience, or bearing witness (Herman, 1997; Hoffman, 2011).

SUMMARY OF CHAPTERS

In chapter 2, I establish an understanding of creativity and play as developmental potentials, with a simultaneous emphasis on theoretical and scientific bases of understanding. This chapter is organized into three main sections. First, I describe the theoretical work of Winnicott, which serve as a frame for the binding together of play, creativity, and healing of traumatic material. This is accomplished by investigating the relationship between Winnicott's (1965) idea of potential space and creative emergence; the use of transitional phenomena as a creative intercession for processing trauma to increase deliberative rumination; the role of decathection and catharsis, in which spontaneous play yields expression for agency and affective processing; and the importance of recovering a sense of pleasure in creative action that awakens senses that have been co-opted by trauma. Further, the importance of spontaneous expression in psychodynamic theory, akin to Winnicott, was described in relevance to the multiple domains of experience in which PTG occurs.

Second, I illuminate definitions of creativity in order to present readers with a robust view of this capacity. For this elaboration of creativity, I rely on both the developmental research and theory of Sandra Russ (1993; 2004; 2014) and the work of Winnicott (1971). The definition of play emphasized kinship with creativity as both a developmental capacity and therapeutic aid. Together, creativity and play are not viewed as separate processes, but as mutually sharpening potentials.

Third, the varieties of creative expression in the psychological literature are explored in conversation with their usefulness as adjunctive therapeutic processes, with suggestions for individualized application. Research in music, dance, drama, and visual arts therapy was briefly reviewed. This is accomplished in dialogue with Lusebrink and Hinz's (2016) Expressive Therapies Continuum (ETC), which is then reflected back to the theoretical stance of Winnicott (1971), who used creative manifestations of play as a route to healing and emergence of the true self. The sense of selfhood, wholeness, spontaneity, and pleasure that creativity has elicited was tied back within the wider framework of Herman's (1997) stages of remembrance/mourning and reconnection with life. The concept of growth within this framework served as a primer to introduce a theological view of creativity.

Chapter 3 is divided into three sections in order to provide a theological account of creativity. I begin with a recounting of what it means to be made in the image of God, highlighting the scriptures and creation story in Genesis 1–3 and detailing the themes of creation out of chaos, and unique, loving relationship as central to humanity's beginning. Such themes are paralleled in the work of Winnicott as a bridge to clinical integration with faith (Ulanov, 2005).

Second, the emphasis on play as an act of recovery of holistic freedom is discussed. This is accomplished by using the work of theologian Jürgen Moltmann, concerning the theology of play as liberation (Moltmann et al., 1972). I also include an account of the Spirit's presence in sustaining life, and the power of experiencing awe and wonder as part of abundant living (Moltmann, 1992). Further, Moltmann's view of play, which has remained grounded in Easter Freedom, serves to connect creative expression as a theologically meaningful aspect in the restoration of selfhood, within contexts of trauma.

Third, a sense of freedom, awe, and wonder in renewed experiences of creativity, is extended to practices within the community of the Church. This is likened to Herman's prominent focus on the role of bearing witness to traumatic experience, which can also become a theological witness of solidarity and hope when held within a loving and spirited community. Theoretical and practical applications are delineated for Christians in relationship with and supporting one another.

In chapter 4, I provide a foundation for the specific connection between creative experience and PTG by tracing the history, internal structure, and theory behind PTG, and overtly linking the mechanisms of change in PTG with creative activity. I begin by elaborating upon the impact of trauma, including the incidence of clinical and subclinical trauma in epidemiological studies, and include a description of the varieties of trauma.

Next, the relationship between posttraumatic stress and PTG is discussed in the context of Herman's (1997) framework, and included an outline of the five core domains of PTG (Calhoun & Tedeschi, 2013). Then, the physiological correlates between art therapy and trauma are expounded, focusing on the impact of hemispheric lateralization and integration (Van der Kolk, 2003), narrative and trauma (Pennebaker, 1997; Pennebaker & Beall, 1986; Pennebaker & Chung, 2012), and art therapy and trauma treatment (King, 2016). The inclusion of the physiological correlates, narrative formation, and utility of art therapy in trauma treatment provide an anchor for understanding the potential relationships between the domains of PTG, the mind, and the body in the creative process.

Finally, the mechanisms of change within the construct of PTG are connected to the functionality of creative expression. This includeds the role of expert companionship; the role of meaning making and constructive self-disclosure; and the importance of building deliberative forms of rumination over intrusive forms functioning as a mechanism. Together, suggestions are given to increase ways in which clients and their therapists could collaboratively buffer creative agency and reclaim a sense of play, as a formative route toward multidimensional growth.

In chapter 5, I restate the thesis and prompt readers for both clinical and ecumenical engagement for accessing creativity as a method of enhancing the possibility of PTG, from a standpoint of Christian faith. This chapter is structured by using the *adenium obesum* or desert rose, to symbolize the layers of change and growth that can occur through creativity and play, which is immersed in theological meaning. The symbol of the desert rose—and each corresponding layer of existence from the soil, roots, trunk, flowers, and oxygenation—is used to playfully communicate through symbols, with respect to the work of Winnicott (1971). This is meant to provide tangible representation of how deep change can work through time, space, relationships, and the nutrients of God's presence in the world, as well as also manifesting implications concerning the use of creative expression in the context of trauma.

2

Theories of Creativity and Play in Human Development

THE CURRENT CHAPTER SERVES as an introduction to a theory of creativity as described by Winnicott (1971), with a particular focus on the roles of play and human connection in eliciting authentic creative expression. This theoretical perspective is integrated with the existing research in developmental scaffolding of creative processes, to provide both empirical and theoretical foundations cultivating creativity. Finally, practical avenues of creative articulation are provided, to illustrate different creative forms that could enhance a variety of therapeutic and growth-oriented experiences in respect to trauma.

In order to accomplish this, I begin the current chapter by investigating creativity through the psychoanalytic theory of Winnicott. Winnicott's understanding of creative activity in relationship to play, selfhood, and the impact of trauma, was extended to guide the rest of the chapter. This included describing Winnicott's (1965; 1971) concept of *potential space* in context of the individual's artistic or creative medium, as well as the forms of *transitional phenomena*—which are the actual material that an individual creates. Further, the role of pleasure and embodied play in the development of the self were expounded. Together these themes inform a broad theory of creativity, as well as offer a vision of potential for trauma recovery from a Winnicottian perspective.

Next, creativity is addressed from a developmental perspective. This emerged from a definition of creativity that, for the purposes of this study, is rooted in formative experiences of play in childhood, again leaning on the clinical work of Winnicott (1971), as well as the reflections of Piaget (1945), and the comprehensive research of Russ (2014). As creative experiences increase in complexity throughout the process of learning and maturation, play and creativity can be understood as mutually sharpening experiences that exist in dialectical relationship to the growth process.

After extending a Winnicottian vision of creativity and reflecting on the role of creativity in psychological development, various modalities of creative expression are explored. This includeds interaction with current studies in the creative fields—such as music, dance, and fine arts—highlighting their relationship to both psychological health and trauma treatment. This background provideds opportunity for dialogue with Lusebrink and Hinz (2016) ETC, a proposed model tailored to the modalities of creative expression for each individual's trauma recovery.

DEFINITIONS OF CREATIVITY

Understanding the creative process, let alone defining the breadth of "creativity" has been historically elusive, debated and described in wide-ranging perspectives (see Sawyer, 2006; Torrance, 1965). The nuanced and differentiated views of creativity that have appeared throughout history have revealed something about the dynamic nature of creative thought, in and of itself. One pivotal example can be seen within the perspective of ancient Greek writers who held a "mystical" understanding of creativity, which emphasized "musing," "genius," inspiration, and transcendence (Negus & Pickering, 2002, p. 90). Such views have shaped an understanding of creativity which would materialize centuries later, reverberating in deep dialogue with the Platonic to form an understanding of creativity as "muse." Plato viewed creativity as a force of direct divine inspiration, which was an imitative reflection of the flawless realm of ideal forms and reason (Sawyer, 2006). Implicitly, this view held definitive sway, especially regarding creative works which were seen as monumental, exceptional, and explicitly culture-shaping. However, with the advent of psychology steeped in the scientific process, an approach to creativity as "muse" has become partially demystified. Yet, even with the utility of explicit scientific studies and the implementation of formalized hypotheses testing, understanding creative potential has remained vast, cumbersome, and in many cases, mysterious.

More recently in the field of psychological science, the varied definitions of creativity have been a matter of continued debate given the plethora of interwoven cognitive, affective, and physiological processes required to generate something deemed creative (Hennesey & Amabile, 2010; Kaufman & Gregoire, 2015). In an effort to narrow and operationalize creativity for scientific purposes, scholar E. Paul Torrance (1965), described it as "the process of becoming sensitive to problems, deficiencies, gaps in knowledge, missing elements, disharmonies . . . searching for solutions . . . testing and retesting them . . . and finally communicating the results" (p. 663–64).

Even from a distance, it became clear that Torrance's particular creative process as a psychological scientist in the era of the 1960s, may have strongly impacted his definition of creativity. Torrance was mostly describing the creative problem-solving process of a research scientist. But for the abstract painter searching to communicate the tension of existence; the hip-hop producer searching to recover musical roots while lyrically enlisting the social problems of the present; or the child dramatizing his or her favorite animal while playing with friends, the former definition of creativity has remained extremely limited, if almost irrelevant. In order to accurately capture the breadth of creative experience, there must be a more holistic approach to the way in which creativity is defined.

A more recent, psychologically minded description offered by Sternberg (2003), emphasized creativity as the ability to initiate original, "novel," "useful," and "high quality" work (p. 89). This definition has allowed for a wide space of application; yet still signified strong contextual, and sociocultural interpretation of what would be considered useful, original, and of high quality. Such a definition has denoted a higher value on the perception of the product, rather than the meaning and genuine emotions knit into and out of creative space. This limitation has impacted the ways in which creative potential can be defined. In an attempt to be rational, it seems that psychological researchers have potentially neglected the subjective and developmental importance of creative expression. The subjective side has reflected both the unique personhood of the person creating and the potentially symbolic meaning embedded in the creations of an individual.

The subjective aspect of creative work has entailed a re-working of muse that is mundane, accessible to everyone, but also distinctly reflective of individuality. A primarily reductionist empiricism can oversimplify the inherent complexity in creativity and the process as it unfolds (Csikszentmihalyi, 1996). An objective definition of creativity centered on the utility and ingenuity of products, as provided by Sternberg (2003), should also respect the subjective elements of creativity that have brought personal meaning to arts, literature, music, and other creative forms. Psychoanalyst Winnicott's work has illuminated a personal and formative depth to the creative process, which was not solely focused on the external aspects of creativity, but emphasized the personal power of playful exploration.

WINNICOTT, EMBODIED EXPRESSION, AND PSYCHOANALYTIC THEORY

Winnicott has provided a natural theoretical link between play and creativity, and has also inspired the capacity for each to promote psychological growth. He suggested that play and creative expression were resources toward self-understanding, healing, and growth. Winnicott's theory has provided a framework for personal expansion beyond traumatic experience, as will be discussed later. D. W. Winnicott, a unique figure in the psychoanalytic school of British Object Relations, was known for taking a moderate stance between the competing ideologies of Anna Freud and Melanie Klein. Although this moderate stance brought a new vision in his understanding of psychological development, his work was sometimes difficult to digest given his frequent coining of novel terms concerning both the human psyche and the therapeutic situation (Grolnick, 1990; Mitchell & Black, 1995). But what was perhaps most unique about the origins of Winnicott's theory of psychological development, especially given the era he was writing in, was that it was charged with compassionate relationality.

For Winnicott, love was the main ingredient required for a self to truly develop. This love began in the symbiotic bond between mother and infant, and was strengthened through a "good enough mother" who was attuned to the infant's experiences—providing safety, care, and holding (Winnicott, 1971, p. 13). Good-enough mothering is the normative, but deep, resonating care that naturally occurs through a steady loving gaze, and basic responsiveness to an infant's physical and emotional needs, without impinging upon the infant's experience by frequent miscues, strong external affects (i.e., anxiety or withdrawal), or physical neglect. Good-enough mothering sets the foundation for the baby to internalize a solidified sense of self, and to thrive in the freedom that such basic, but powerful attuned care brings (Mitchell & Black, 1995).

The type of immersive, subjective giving that Winnicott's good-enough mother (or primary caretaker) provided before an infant has actual objective power and is completely vulnerable, is the very same powerful giving that cultivates self-efficacy later in development. Stephen Mitchell (1995) summarized Winnicott's emphasis on "primary maternal preoccupation" as a symbiotic relationship in which the caretaker "shapes the world around the child so as to fulfill that . . . relational and embodied . . . desire" (p. 126). This experience prepares a child with a sense of subjective omnipotence (an illusionary sense of personal power in the world) through the caretaker's responsiveness to the baby's spontaneous needs, actions, and expressions. It provides an inherent sense of being able to create experience, though illusionary at first, that builds a basic trust in life required to mature holistically.

However, it is also important that the mother not be intrusive when she is not needed, and so she must provide "a psychical space within which the infant is protected without knowing [they are] protected" (Mitchell & Black, 1995, p. 126), which Winnicott (1971) refers to as the holding environment. The holding environment is the environment which "good-enough" therapy ought to emulate, as to provide the individual with a corrective refuge to resume psychic development. In the chronic absence of an adequate holding environment, an infant or child is prone to develop a state of disorder where the "false self" dominates over the "true self."

The true self is viscerally connected to the original "wellsprings of desire and meaning," whereas the false self is disconnected out of "premature, forced necessity" to deal with external triggers (i.e., anxiety of abandonment or overwhelming intrusion; Mitchell & Black, 1995, p. 131). Winnicott scholar Simon Grolnick (1990) described the true self as "expression of an inner, sensorimotor, gut self" (p. 32), that naturally occurs when a caretaker is holding and validating an infant or toddler's experience through empathic mirroring of their feelings, desires, frustrations and pleasures. In the process of holding and mirroring, psychological safety is established and the "true self" comes out to "play" in spontaneous, lively discovery, experimentation, and energy.

The false self, presents through the opposite experience—mainly a constricting, misattuned, or even dangerous environment, where a caretaker persistently fails to mirror, empathize or attune to an infant or toddler's experience. To compensate for this lack of validation, the infant or toddler will develop a "false self" which conforms to the experience of a constricting, ignoring, or even hostile environment. In adulthood, the false self presents as a continuum of social and even neurotic conformity and collusion, where a person's genuine feelings, thoughts and desires are repressed, denied or ignored. For Winnicott, access to the "true self" is a therapeutic activity, because it is free, and unhindered by neuroses, and usually would manifest in play and creative life (Grolnick, 1990; Winnicott, 1971).

Creative play is one of the ways in which an individual can learn to connect with the true self, which is founded in that spontaneous, original activity that occurs in holding (Winnicott, 1954; Winnicott, 1965; Winnicott, 1971). For example, a toddler who is separated from a warm and attuned caretaker may become preoccupied with the caretaker's absence in moments, stifling their own energy to play and discover the environment. But when a toddler's caretaker returns and is able to re-establish the safety of an emotional bond, this reinforces a sense of containment that allows the child to begin "playing"; perhaps this is with sticks, pots and pans, or other household objects. In exploring the texture, weight, sound, and color a child's imagination becomes involved in an experimental process with the external objects. But what the child is also discovering in those moments, is their own agency, their own motor skills, mimetic power, and imaginative capacity. It is a spontaneous occurrence that brings life, pleasure, and an expanding sense of self together.

This is why Winnicott (1971) stated that "the playing has to be spontaneous, and not compliant or acquiescent, if psychotherapy is to be done" (p. 68). Creativity is the natural extension of play that occurs in between the self, and the outer environment, which Winnicott (1971) called "potential space" (p. 135). The potential space is the field in which the formation of personality and experience can develop, especially through play and creative explorations. This potential space exists as a resource for therapeutic healing which can manifest through specific occurrences, symbols, and interactions which help a forming person reconcile their internal world with external reality called "transitional phenomena." Potential space and transitional phenomena will be further defined and described in additional detail in the following sections. In a good-enough holding environment an emergent space is created, in which the true self may be able to flourish while the false self is allowed to recede, and channels of joy and bodily pleasure are able to be experienced anew.

Winnicott's theory is holistic in the sense that both healing and growth are underscored by the same transformative, embodied approach to psychological formation. The primary conceptual links in Winnicott's work between play and creativity are that of potential space, transitional phenomena, and pleasure/embodiment. The role of each of these concepts intersect in a larger psychoanalytic perspective that provide a bridge between the self and the creative process. Further, these concepts also inform an approach to healing towards traumatic experience, and growth. Even though Winnicott's definition of trauma is focused on the subjective developmental experiences that impede the formation of self, this theory still has vital contributions towards the framework for trauma recovery provided by Judith Herman (1997).

Herman scaffolds the healing process first from safety, then to an understanding of the trauma (she calls grief/mourning) then finally, moves to reconnection. In the following chapters, Herman's frame will be discussed in greater detail, but the key element for connecting to Winnicott is the way that she structures psychological treatment of trauma to move from a foundation of immediate personal safety, toward greater internalization of empathy toward one's self, and eventually new experiences and life. Winnicott highlights that the scaffolding of new experience to occur through potential space, transitional phenomena and pleasurable bodily connection to self, that can continue to grow throughout a person's lifetime. Herman traces an arc of recovery that occurs first through safety and refuge, secondly through the processing of emotions, memories and pain through grief and mourning, and finally through reconnective and reconstructed elements of living that are restorative. Winnicott's ideas can provide a theoretical infusion of creativity and psychic transformation into Herman's framework, through his concepts of potential space, transitional phenomena, and pleasure.

Potential Space

Potential space is the area that exists between subjective and objective realities. In infancy, subjective experience is fused with an inherent vulnerability that can become quickly terrifying, given that there is complete dependence on caretakers for physical and emotional needs. Such a primitive state—though so vulnerable—is also a harbor for the incredible growth that occurs at this stage of development. The outside world can become quickly overwhelming, but given enough experience with good-enough mothering and a holding environment, more subjective power and safety are gradually internalized.

This potential space, begins as the relational field of connection that fluctuates between infant and mother; but over the course of development extends to the space between the child and the family, the adolescent and society, and the adult and the full range of the outer world. Winnicott states that all of this potential space "depend on experience which leads to trust . . . [and] can be looked upon as sacred to the individual in that it is here that the individual experiences creative living" (1971, p. 139). On the foundation of internalized trust, individuals experience the freedom to express themselves without impingement from another, and so learn to connect their body, emotions and curiosity in a way that leads to exploration of the outer elements, physical space, and the psychological subjectivity of others. Potential space is the "in between" place where a child can grow in psychological development, learning feelings, actions and communications are their own, and what belongs to other people, and the outside environment. A sense of self, a sense of others, and a basic trust in the world can integrate in this potential space.

Potential space is also the place of experimentation, or psychological "canvas" where the true self can become consolidated through congruent, meaningful and even pleasurable experiences. Later in development this may include the creative mediums in a general sense—such as architecture, music, and the forms of culture and religion. Potential space is the environment awaiting to be filled with unique modes of communication, experimentation and even consolidated in work. For Winnicott (1971) disorder reflects the inability to live creatively, that looks practically like a "poverty of play and cultural life" (p. 147). In such poverty the false self dominates, because there is a core inability to be able to trust in the self in relation to the environment. The potential space that could yield meaningful and enjoyable play and work, becomes constricted due to this lack of an adequate holding environment.

Potential space is a metaphor for the safe and loving environment a caretaker provides, which allows the development of a child's embodied self-efficacy to grow, the sense of self-trust and self-discovery in increase, and gradual ability to trust in the outside world flourish. A child who uses the potential space which is exists in the field of an attuned loving bond, allows the authentic, true self to manifest, and can release a need to develop and maintain a false self to placate external constriction. The true self thrives in the love, safety, and attunement which can become internalized, eventually enabling the child to access, tolerate and accept their own emotions, bodily experiences, and longings. This emergence of authentic experiencing is what can continue blossom within potential space, supporting a child's ability to connect with, and act from, the true self.

Therapeutically speaking, potential space is also a place where the past, present and spontaneous possibility of the future can meet: it is a place in between subjective fantasy and objective reality that allows for transitional experience (Ben Ezer, 2012; Winnicott, 1971). In therapy, potential space allows for new experience to occur, and old experience to be integrated through a return to trusting the self and the outside world with a sense of contentment and "continuity" (Grolnick, 1990, p. 30) that happens within a context of safety and holding. This sense of continuity is the freedom to be, and intuitively know that one is held in loving attention. Winnicott (1971) calls this state of continuity "going on being," which is the freedom and autonomy stemming from healthy, internalized experiences of dependence.

The interplay between of old experience of dependence and new experiences of autonomy and exploration is what it is referred to as "transitional." That is, old experiences are the internalized experiences of object relations, which guide new developmental experiences in interactions with the outside world. New experiences of autonomy, and independence are essential to form memories, sensations, thoughts and relationships, that not only shape healthy emotional development, but also introduce surprises in all these areas that bring the vitality of joy and discovery. Unfortunately, during developmental trauma, old experiences of dependence may have been impinging, caustic and painful; influencing the dependent child (or adult) to repress, dismiss or even dissociate their genuine feelings, responses or relational connections. The result of repetitive traumatic, or strongly impinging encounters is developmental stagnation.

One example would be when a primary caregiver displays too much depression, anxiety and dissociation from their own untreated trauma—perhaps like an acute experience of witnessing cultural/political genocide in Rwanda or Cambodia—which causes the caregiver to be unable to provide containment, mirroring or empathy for their child. The caregiver's own pain interrupts the flow of relational connection and safety, which the child internalizes or interprets in their fully dependent state as unsafe. This might result in the child either developing a false self, to appease the caregiving object, at the cost of their own experience; dismissing, avoiding, repressing, or even dissociating their own affects through the various experience of a caregiver's trauma (Mitchell & Black, 1995).

However, if the caretaker is able to maintain an empathic, safe and attuned connection with the child in spite of their painful past, that reinforces a sense of psychological and physical safety in the child. The true self is able to come out and play, because the good-enough holding environment has been provided. A lack physical safety, in the context of cultural or environmental turmoil—be it poverty, war, crime, disease, famine—can also cause impingement that is wider and more diffuse in scope, constraining the ability to play. So, an adequate holding environment might also extend to the realm of physical safety. However, a healthy psychological bond with one significant person, or the holding space of a specific community, may be enough to help form adaptive forms of play even when environmental resources are scarce. Whether impingement is primarily psychic or physical, the context of emotional and physical safety is the nesting place for health, given that mind and body are inextricably connected.

New experiences of a good-enough holding environment can helps form a potential space, where new, more authentic and whole experiences can be developmentally integrated into their sense of self while interacting in, and with, the world. In everyday life, this new experience within potential space can take the wider form of culture, work environment, artistic endeavors or recreational activity, and continued "transitional" (developmental) experience could truthfully occur within any of these contexts. Therapy, however is a concentrated place for transitional experience to occur, because through the therapeutic relationship, regression, "unintegration and discontinuity" (Mitchell & Black, 1995, p. 133) can occur in a way that allows more primitive emotional and unconscious material to arise in a place of emotional containment. The therapeutic alliance becomes a facilitating factor towards creative living, but also to healing wounds which may be hidden or developmental trauma that may have fractured a person's ability to get in touch with their true self (Winnicott, 1971).

This potential space provides an opportunity for the primal effects of an individual's internal world to meet external reality in a developmentally congruent way, that helps to integrate meaningful feelings, thoughts and actions together. In the absence of traditional psychoanalytic therapy requiring multiple sessions each week, or as an adjunct to therapy, an artistic canvas, musical instrument, dance stage, or blank sheet of writing paper may function as an asset to the foundation of potentiality that Winnicott describes. Such a creative space might give rise to movement from inner fantasy toward creative agency, and ultimately, self-discovery, which will be further described in the proceeding sections. Of course, an individualized network of safety must be intact to move forward in creative exploration—there must be a tie, or bond to some trustworthy other, hopefully a licensed therapist, social worker or "expert companion" as described by Calhoun and Tedeschi (2013). In addition, the individual must have a baseline ability to employ self-soothing and regulating techniques, in the case that the emotionality of creativity overrides their stress tolerance (Herman, 1997; Ogden et al., 2006; Siegel, 1999).

There are many creative mediums that may serve as potential space. Painting alone might provide creative mediums of acrylic, oil, and watercolor; while music could provide the mediums of jazz, blues, and country. Different personalities may gravitate towards a particular medium that resonates with their expressive interests, allowing for communication of the self which is particularly meaningful. Within the potential space of a canvas, a painter may decide to use the thick and rich base of oil, with an abstract symbolism. A music connoisseur on the other hand, might find folk music through the instrumental medium of a mandolin to provide a personally charged expressive pathway. Such potential space provided by the canvas, medium, or instrument, allows distinct unconscious and conscious forms to present themselves.

Transitional Phenomena

If creative mediums function as a therapeutic potential space, the material that is spontaneously generated within that space may become what is known as "transitional phenomena." Transitional phenomena are the symbolic material that promotes psychological integration, by allowing dormant material to manifest externally (Winnicott, 1971). Often, Winnicott found that in spontaneous moments of play, unique symbols of psychopathology would manifest vividly—particularly in ways that the client did not have linguistic or conscious access to. Whether this was through narration of disturbing dreams, drawings, or the peculiar use of blocks, strings, and paper accessible in his office, fantasies would find playful outlets to express inner conflict and unmet needs.

But interpretation of fantasy symbols was not the end of the road for Winnicott. Instead the play process itself was simultaneously an agent of healing and a route to a sense of self. Winnicott (1971) stated that

> in a search of the self the person concerned may have produced something valuable in terms of art, but a successful artist may be universally acclaimed and yet to have failed to find the self that he or she is looking for. (p. 73)

This quote characterizes his value for the true self as bodily, emotional, and authentic in the physical act of creating. The purpose of creativity is not social-esteem, though this is undoubtedly a shaping force in the potential space of culture, but is genuine meaning extended to the outside world. These creative activities—or, possible transitional experiences—often occur in symbolic representations—whether the medium is string, paint, song, wood, steel, bodily movement or social symbol.

In *Playing and Reality* (Winnicott, 1971) this symbolic material, again, is referred to as transitional phenomena. Often early in childhood, transitional phenomena take place through specific physical objects, called transitional objects. Winnicott explains that transitional objects such as a blanket, toy, or stuffed animal, function as a symbolic source of safety and nurturance with which children have tied to their caretakers. The blanket, stuffed animal or toy is a stand-in for their caretaker, which are discovered through play. These early symbols help children feel connected to "mother" as they explore the world, and also have the power to reconcile subjective, inner needs with the overwhelming presence of the objective outer world. In essence, a transitional object "is what we see of this journey of progress towards experiencing" (Winnicott, 1971, p. 8). It is the "intermediate area of experience, between thumb and teddy bear, between the oral eroticism and the true object-relationship, between primary creative activity and projection of what has already been introjected" (Winnicott, 1953, p. 89). The transitional object itself serves as an externalized form of psychological integration, helping reconcile a child's inner needs through an external, tangible representation. This integration of mutual affects of aggression and dependence, and desires for agency with fears of the outer world, can be contained through the transitional object, which represents a caretaker's holding in a physical symbol.

Even though such an object is "illusory"—from the standpoint that the stuffed animal is not actually a real caretaker—the actual object's function is immensely practical. The projected safety infused into a physical symbol which represents safe harbor, and a tangible container for ebbing and flowing dependence, propels eventual moments of new autonomy. The tie to the stuffed animal or toy which the child has "created" by projecting their emotional needs onto, through their imagination, reminds the child that they are safe to play, explore and discover. Such autonomy occurs in moments in which a child can access their spontaneous, creative self apart from their primary caretaker, and live out psychic health. A transitional object jump-starts the memory of a holding environment and offers refuge for the "true self," which is the spontaneous personality that emerges in the safety of love. For a toddler, a loving, "good enough" tie to the primary caregiver, brings the security to be authentic, genuine, and playful. In lieu of the caregiver, and later in development, a transitional object functions as a temporary stand-in for the caregiver. A simple example would be a toddler who carries her stuffed polar bear with her when she is babysat by grandparents, or relatives. The stuffed polar bear serves as a tie to her primary caretakers, and helps soothe the anxiety of being in a less established environment, and helps them to safely transition to a new, less familiar environment.

This type of phenomena can help an individual continue living in present experience, rather than escaping through physical or emotional distance, splitting or even shut-down (Winnicott, 1953). When a child, or even adult, is able to access their authentic self through the safe connection and memory symbolized in a transitional object, they can internalize more emotional stability within themselves, making it easier to explore the world beyond their caretaker, or primary attachment figure. But as an individual matures psychologically, the need for such an object is decreased, and a child's "primary creativity" is not overwhelmed by "objective perception" (Winnicott, 1971, p. 15), and instead can be expressed consciously through avenues of culture, art and religion.

Winnicott (1971) held that the primary creativity that begins with transitional objects, is not fully relinquished in maturation, but instead moves outward in new forms (transitional phenomena) that may even contribute to society. For example, such as the customs and rituals of food and games in culture (i.e., sports, festivals), art (i.e., patterns, styles, form, color), and religion (i.e., songs, liturgy, prayer forms, symbols/icons) can all represent an extension of personal meaning and expression that is also grounded in a primitive need for containment, and security (Grolnick, 1990). For Winnicott, culture, art and religion are mature forms of transitional phenomena;

but adults may still need a place to express more primitive needs to deal with times of disruption, insecurity, or traumatic experience. This place, for an adult, can be accessed through primary creativity, to help bring meaning and coherence to their transitional needs.

Winnicott (1971) also held that during maturation, "transitional objects become gradually decathected" (p. 19), meaning that the child has been able integrate the symbolic meaning enough that the toy or stuffed animal is no longer needed. However, some experiences in adulthood may require a reintegration or catharsis that functions as a mature return to transitional phenomena for healing and repair. Adult decathection and catharsis may help individuals navigate internal and external chaos, through a return to "being" or spontaneous activity, with the help of transitional phenomena (i.e., creativity; Outeiral, 2013). An example could be a pottery sculpture, in which an individual increasingly learns to sculpt a stylish cup or bowl from clay. At one level, this may represent an expression of learning to provide for oneself—the bowl or cup is representative of a dependent state for food, shelter, or eating utensils—but at another level the personalization in the styling of the cup or bowl may be layered and ornamented with colors or hues that represent their affect, integrating dyes of red and blue into a purple, that connotes a calm, but erotic tone.

Such a sculpture is practical but also emotionally representative of the individual's process and maturation. Adult decathection it is an exercise in which human limits and human expression occur in tandem. Clay is tangible, yet moldable. Color is particular, but changeable. Immersion in such creative expressive acts, include the learning curve of working with finite tools, in a finite world. For Winnicott, healthy maturation involves creative expression, which incites a core wisdom in clients who are working through times of identity crises, loss, confusion, fear, and even trauma. This wisdom, which stems from the experience of the true self, occurs through the agency, and freedom of play, which yields creative life.

Pleasure

Creative transitional phenomena offer a sounding board for affects which have been split off, desires that are latent, or narrative that is dormant in the unconscious (Ulanov, 2005). In this way creativity can offer access to fuller experience, physical agency, and spontaneous play, that fosters an integrated return to the objective world. But play and creativity can also provide a very basic, but powerful human experience—that of pleasure. By connecting through one's body, and experiencing pleasure in the act of creating, individuals can use potential space and transitional phenomena as a salve to a variety of psychological needs.

Winnicott (1971) reminded therapists that "the absence of psycho-neurotic illness may be health, but it is not life" (p. 134). Life is bodily, and bodily experience is central to organizing a coherent sense of self. This is why play must be "essentially satisfying," "exciting" and "precarious" (Winnicott, 1971, p. 70). The power of satisfaction and pleasure in play is captured in more recent therapies, like Accelerated Experiential Dynamic Therapy (Fosha, 2009). Fosha contended that an emotion like pleasure that comes from mastery and self-expression is an "adaptive action tendency" (p. 177), which can match and help transform disrupting affects, as emotions are processed. As an individual is able to express or communicate in a form that is fundamentally pleasing to the senses, this could facilitate emotional processing in a way that leads to emergent experiences that might not only be healing, but reorienting to a sense of vitality like what occurs in Winnicott's description of the reemergence of the true self.

However, it is not appropriate to equate physiological pleasure with creativity and healing. Rather, the emergence of pleasure occurs within a network of other experiences, like self-efficacy, joy and contentment that make it beneficial (Fosha, 2009). This may be why Winnicott emphasized that play should not be overtly "erotogenic," because over-stimulation of erogenous areas can trigger too intense an experience of primitive merging, which interferes with the sense of agency and differentiation that is pivotal to play, and the creative experience, which implicitly would differentiate transitional phenomena from something like thumb-sucking, or masturbation. Though it would be inaccurate to fully equate play and creativity with physical pleasure, pleasure is still an integrative element that can encourage development and motivation.

This theory of pleasure in play harmonizes with scholar Mihaly Csikzentmihalyi's observation that in order to sustain creativity, it must also be enjoyable (1996). Csikzentmihalyi spent years studying creative individuals who entered into highly demanding work without much pay, including "chess players, rock climbers, dancers, and composers" (p. 111). Some commonalities he found for what made such activities so enjoyable, were the element of challenge, physical activity combined with heightened awareness, absence of fear of failure, lack of self-consciousness, and that these activities become "autotelic"—meaning that activities are enjoyed for their own sake—not for the product at the end. These aspects of creative enjoyment portray a sense of immersion in experience that unites personal meaning and physical agency. This is very similar to the type of criteria Winnicott sets forth for qualifying play as therapeutic.

However, Csikzentmihalyi also found an element of progressive and clear goal-directedness common to creative enjoyment, which differs from Winnicott's view. Yet this goal-directedness that individuals found so enjoyable, appears to be related to the pleasure of developing a craft. The gradual improvement in the ability to know that one is making progress in terms of their craft, might also indicate that their self-expression within a particular "potential space" can become more robust over time.

The power of transitional phenomena and the experience of pleasure in play brings together multiple layers of human psychological experience that can connect in acts of creativity. The combination of safety, unconscious communication, emergent affect, and implicit self-narratives that might surround the creative process and could provide individuals in distress with a potential space for integrating hardship with authentic desire. Authentic desire is the natural current of Winnicott's (1971) true self, where feelings of dependence, adventure, aggression and tender attention towards others coexist in a relational field of growth. Particularly, the experiential elements embedded in play and creativity might apply toward recovery from traumatic experiences, simultaneously accessing aspects of both healing and growth.

Creativity, Trauma, and Recovery

Although the roles of play and creativity in psychological development are multifaceted, their roles in recovery from traumatic distress may also have powerful relevance. The relationship between creative expression and improvement after clinical and subclinical experiences of trauma have been established empirically in the psychological literature (Crenshaw, 2006; Garland et al., 2007; Hass-Cohen, 2008; Hass-Cohen & Findlay, 2015; Koss & Trantham, 2013; Malchiodi & Crenshaw, 2013). But the nuances of how creative expression functions as a healing agent is difficult to capture, and will benefit from theoretical and empirical study. Winnicott's theory of both trauma and of creativity intersect to guide application to trauma recovery that include the holding environment, transitional objects, and embodied expression (Ulanov, 2005).

When individuals come to therapy—especially after traumatic experience—there can be an essential need for basic psychic holding. In regards to acute trauma, Judith Herman, reflects this sentiment in the stage of Safety—which implies a need for enough affective and physiological tolerance to actually move into the explicit content of therapy, safeguarding the risk of triggering panic, re-experienced terror and even dissociation (1997). For survivors of trauma, this is establishing a baseline of collaborative interventions that keeps the fight or flight response from completely taking over the therapeutic space, often through stepwise de-escalation techniques like grounding, deep-breathing, that attend to the individual's "window of tolerance" (Siegel, 1999). At a more generic level, the stage of safety that employs interpersonal trust, and interventions for de-escalating the traumatic stress response, is similar to Winnicott's emphasis on establishing a holding environment in therapy. In effect, it is the holding environment, which includes attuned presence and safety, that precedes the emergent, and "creative" aspects of therapy. Such an environment, or that acutely envisioned by Herman's stage of establishing safety by building self-regulatory skills, eventually gives rise to what Winnicott refers to as "potential space." Bonamino and DiRenzo (2000) stated that "the process of establishing a potential space . . . where traumatic events that could not be previously experienced can then be included and integrated into the play or dream . . . [and] traumas can finally assume a personal and idiomatic emotional meaning for the self" (p. 112). Trauma, for Winnicott is the pervasive impingement that stagnates development and creativity. The safe boundaries of a contained space allow an individual to divulge the urgency of their needs, and if met with attuned emotional affect and mirroring in therapy, healthy adaptation to the demands of the world can occur (Modell, 1976; Winnicott, 1965).

Traumatic exposure can interrupt a person's sense of safety, rupturing the fragility of the childlike level of dependence and state of "going on being," that is so vital to developing a coherent sense of self (Winnicott, 1971). In order to navigate such triggers and maintain coherent sense of self without cueing a panicked or dissociative response, an individual often requires concrete access to symbols of safety—like a transitional object (Ulanov, 2005). Transitional objects can function as a symbol of safety for a developing child (or adult) to mediate their need to hold onto a representative space of safety and comfort, providing a psychological tether to that safety, so they cannot venture out into the everyday world with a sense of agency and soothing. Even though a transitional object is meant to be outgrown, the function of such an object can bring rich insight for those negotiating pain, grief, and readjustment to a world which has become fraught with terrifying triggers. This is why Winnicott (1953) describes that transitional objects typically elicit some level of control or "subjective omnipotence," and must "survive instinctual loving, and also hating" as pure aggression, in a way that it can both be "excitedly loved and mutilated," as to diffuse the internal feelings into outer diffusion (p. 91). In the subjective (and often objective) helplessness of trauma, personal power, creative agency and emotional and physical safety need to be gradually reclaimed to bring about healing. In order to do this, artistic modes of expression can help integrate the variance of emotional states, through a combination of creative mediums (i.e., potential space; Hass-Cohen & Findlay, 2015). For Winnicott, creativity is key to resuming development after trauma and distress, while fantasy is the escape from development. Creativity is active and self-generated, while fantasy remains in the mind, and untapped for its healing and potential for meaning-making.

The distinction between fantasy as "material that . . . [is] locked in fixity" and creativity, as active "dreaming . . . which is living" marks the gradual discovery of "the living core of the individual personality" (Winnicott, 1971, pp. 42–43). Trauma can create a regressive sense of fixity entrenched with primal fear (Calhoun & Tedeschi, 2013). In the aftermath of trauma, fantasies of destruction and terror can take over the sense of agency, self-control and safety that are harbored in potential space. Movement past the fixity of horrifying, stagnating, and even fracturing tragedy requires courage, support, sensitivity and holistic attention. This therapeutic attention provides the link between mind, body and sense of self, so that "play" in Winnicott's literal and existential sense, can serve as a nurturing medicine. Creative exploration and play promote rediscovered agency, resilience, and solidarity within the self, according to Winnicott's theory (1971). But the play process inevitably requires movement back and forth between harmony and discord.

This should bear some semblance to the role of many canvases, rock anthems, and provocative literature that have gained popularity over the last two hundred years. Harmony and dissonance, order and disorder, narrative and disruption mark the textures of artistic expression that in many ways mirror the micro-traumas and reintegration even of daily human experience. Such polarities become heightened in traumatic aftereffects to the degree that they actually impeded the ability to coherently process emotions, physiology, and even compromise attachment strategies (Klorer, 2016). Again, this is why a well-established holding environment, or sense of safety must first be established before the act of creative expression can yield real benefit. But after this basic safety is scaffolded, transitional phenomena surface in a natural need for expression and a renegotiated sense of exploration, which may be crucial for moving forward in the midst of traumatic after-effects.

A popular example of transitional phenomena could be Tolkien's (1954) *Lord of the Rings*. J. R. R. Tolkien, a soldier and survivor of World War I, and a witness to World War II, experienced the firsthand horrors and the brutality of war. Tolkien's experience may have harkened the role of perseverance, faith in the midst of desperation, the power of creative imagination, and hope in spite of traumatic surroundings (Tolkien, 2017). *Lord of the Rings* is perhaps the most broadly influential work of fiction released in modern times, and illustrates extensive detailed worlds and characters in a tome of creative imagination that includes the role of valor, ferocity, inhibition and fear, timidity, compromise and staunch belief. *Lord of the Rings* integrates a plethora of emotions, characters, and confounding, while illustrating themes of friendship, suffering, hope, character and the journey to a restored, and redeemed world that has been fractured by evil. Tolkien's creativity, however, required a level of physiological safety (that is, the end of his time of deployment in the war) to begin his work, and function as what could be theorized, in part, as transitional phenomena.

Understanding Tolkien's service in World War I brings an empathic understanding to both his personal experience of the trauma of battle, but also the role of restoring creative imagination, once a baseline of safety has been established. It is hard to imagine Tolkien writing in the literal trenches of the first world war, but his functional creativity emerged afterward, within a time that might have been tolerably processed. Tolkien is but one possible figure whose experiences of a globally traumatic environment may have yielded transformative creative expression. An adult form of transitional phenomena, as Tolkien's work might be, is more easily interpreted, than a child's preverbal or developmental trauma which is largely seen in unconscious, bodily forms (Winnicott, 1965; Winnicott, 1971). Yet, Tolkien's imaginary world always carried a childlike sense of possibility and wonder, and is popular evidence of the power of childlike creativity manifest in adulthood (Simpson, 2014; Tolkien, 1966).

PLAY AND CREATIVITY FROM A DEVELOPMENTAL PERSPECTIVE

Given the complexity and weaknesses of defining creativity in a purely attributional way; a more practical, bodily, and developmentally charged definition of creativity as proposed within Winnicott's theory may heighten the impact for both clinical work and theology. A developmental view of creativity is not the exclusive arena of geniuses like Tolkien—though master artists provide some great examples of creativity—but instead has a foundation in childhood. Describing creativity as genius may stagnate its application to everyday people, and may even undermine the personal experiences of play, pleasure, and meaning that may never gain public audience, but provide hidden roots of passion and individuation for many. However, researchers also seem to understand that creativity is strongly connected to originality, and so the study of exceptional characters and traits can guide the understanding of how original creative work evolves. Creative work stems from much more than rote, patterned, and learned behavior (though this guides the development of particular craft, and in socio-cultural context), but contains something simultaneously emergent and deeply personal.

Characteristics of Creativity

So, what does the field of psychology deem to be "creative"? Might this word refer to a general psychological capacity, a personality trait, or a culturally embedded term that simply reflects human agency? It appears that a dutiful understanding of creativity will consider all these factors. Granted, even the study of creativity has been frustrated by difficulties measuring, operationalizing, and conceptually integrating the many layers of perspective which can shape such a wide-ranging, but crucial human ability (Torrance, 1993).

Russ and Wallace (2013) have drawn upon their past studies and the work of Guilford (1950) to do just this. In their wide-ranging research Russ and Wallace characterize creativity in several ways. They include characteristics such as divergent thinking (i.e., cognitive variety in individual ideation), imagination (especially as applied to larger concepts), the use of insight, flexible problem-solving, and being able to take multiple perspectives on a given problem (Russ, 1993; Russ, 2004; Russ, 2014). Divergent thinking and imagination may reflect the subjective, personal, individual elements of thought; while insight, flexible problem-solving, and perspective-taking may reflect the overall elements of intellectual empathy. Together the characteristics of individuality and empathy that guide creativity, as described by Russ and Wallace (2013) align with Murray Bowen's systems-inspired definition of differentiation. Bowen held that differentiation is the ability to maintain one's uniqueness while in relationship (Gilbert, 2006). Differentiation itself, could even been viewed as a creative process.

Csikszentmihalyi (1996) adds to this systems perspective, describing creativity as a contribution that effects or changes culture, in an emergent way. To further flesh out this perspective Csikzentmihalyi describes creativity as the interaction between domain, field, and individual. "Domain" is the particular symbolic form (i.e., Mathematics, Physics, Art, Architecture), "field" is the relational network of those involved (i.e., teachers, practitioners, scholars, agencies), and "individual" is the person contributing using the "symbols of the domain" or even adding a domain (which Csikzentmihalyi likens to Galileo in physics, and Freud in psychoanalysis; p. 28). The complexity of individual contribution, social interpretation, and potential emergent cultural change suggests creative activity as a dynamic process.

With the empirical characteristics, systemic perspectives, and intrapsychic developments involved, it would be easy to get lost in the wide range of scholarly contributions that exist in the study of creativity. For the purposes of this paper's coherence, the word creativity will be less concerned with innovation and perceived ingenuity, and more concerned with the authentic, individual expression that takes place through an embodied, exploratory process of discovery as described by Winnicott (1971) in *Playing and Reality*. This is not to diminish the cultural and sociological ramifications of creativity, but rather to locate the origins of creativity and focus on its potential for personal meaning and growth from a developmental, psychodynamic and clinical perspective. Winnicott's vision of the creativity begins as unique expression of a child exploring an inherently relational environment, in which learning about the self, others and the world occurs spontaneously. Creativity is a function of activity that comes from "being," which naturally occurs in a relationally safe environment. In more simple terms, creativity begins with learning to play.

For Winnicott, play is the foundation of creativity and of personal meaning. And the goal of creativity is not productivity or social esteem —though these can be outgrowths of creativity, and learning to master an art or craft—but to learn to be a unique person in relationship with the outer world (Runco, 2004; Winnicott, 1971). The movement from play to creativity may be accomplished by a variety of underlying psychological processes. Detailing these underlying processes, especially concerning the role of play, may help readers understand how the rich and meaningful varieties of art, literature, culture, architecture and music that fill the world might emerge. Play could be the unintentional "building block" on which creativity is stimulated.

Play and Human Development

While creative works often includes a product, medium, or implicit goal in mind, play often occurs without an explicit "goal," except the goal of enjoyment and being, that stems from trust initially provided by the caretaker (Winnicott, 1971). The emergence of such play occurs in synchrony with many other forms of learning in childhood—including social, environmental, and sensorimotor learning—which can be observed in the sandbox at a park, in coloring and beginning stages of drawing, experimenting with Legos, figurines, and imaginary play with others in playing "war" or "house" (Holmes et al., 2015). The domestic and ideal, rugged and delicate, aggressive and harmonious forms of play common in childhood speak volumes about the development of the emotional, social, and physical processing; and the organic need for synthesis of such developmental material towards an integrated sense of self.

Emotionally, play provides an outlet for feelings to become integrated with thoughts, imagination, and physical energy. Child psychologist and developmental researcher Sandra Russ (2014) notes that a traditional synthesis of psychoanalytic observations emphasize play as primary-process thinking. Primary-process thinking connects pleasure-seeking, with emotional, and bodily energy through outer symbolic activity. This type of play resolves tension between pleasure-seeking, and the medium of the outer world. During play more fluid and flexible ideation emanates, while an array of emotions is accessed, experienced, and/or discharged. Russ contends that this can help children to acclimate to the range of their own emotions, generate greater problem-solving skills through expanded thinking, and cater a degree of emotional pleasure to the experience of resolving the tension that comes from facing challenges (2014). Play may help to synchronize feelings, thoughts, and a degree of external challenge through exploration; yielding a framework for resolving everyday stress that, perhaps many adults would benefit from being able to access within their work life.

This theory is also supported by the empirically informed, systems theory based on differentiation. Observing the breadth of research on optimizing experiences in work and play, Nakamura and Czikszentmihalyi (2009) state that while complexity is often central to creativity, the family system can be a cogent platform for nurturing creativity. The authors found that family systems that most effectively cultivated creativity in their children were characterized by harmonic balance: providing both (a) clear limits/boundaries alongside ample support of individual interests, (b) family time along with and unstructured periods of solitude, (c) and expectations of achievement alongside strong acceptance of failure in experimenting. Such an environment emulates the conditions for developmentally important play suggested by the psychoanalytic position Russ describes, by modeling room for both the individual impulse, desire and drive within a limited context that imposes challenge.

Piaget (1945) believed that though play begins "purely for functional pleasure . . . [and] proceeds by relaxation of effort at adaptation and by maintenance or exercise of activities for the mere pleasure mastering them" (p. 89). Here, play begins in a similar state as the classical psychoanalysts held. But as a child matured, Piaget states that play becomes more difficult to separate from the process of adaptation to the world, and will involve more elements of social imitation. Being a developmental theorist, Piaget suggested that the combinative feedback between play and adaptation occurs in stages, and symbolism reaches "more progressive differentiation between 'signifier' and 'signified'" (p. 101). For Piaget, there are similarities to an analytic perspective of play (though using the language of schema, assimilation and accommodation), but developmentally he employs a multistage framework that accounts for the impact of intellectual and social adaptation in play across the lifespan.

Whether or not Piaget's stages are wholly accurate, his general thesis towards the roles of differentiation, development and environmental adaptation in the play maintain footing in research which suggests the importance of play for both emotional and social development. Hoffman and Russ (2012) found pretend play to be related to emotional regulation, while Howes and Matheson (1992) have also found that complexity of play has been related to higher social competence. Social-drama play has been found to be related linguistic and social-emotional skills (Fisher, 1992); while creativity, social play, and language skills have also been shown to be interrelated (Holmes et al., 2015). However, it has been suggested that such relationships are primarily epiphenomenal—distancing causal inferences between the amount of play and social development (Lillard et al., 2013). Or perhaps, a definition of play that emphasizes primitive intrapsychic meaning, may escape the methodological limitations of measuring such multidimensional and complex process.

In fact, Bodrova, Gemeroth, and Leong (2013) argue that play does not have stronger empirical support, due to diminished quality of play that has occurred for children, with the streamlining of education. Basing their argument on Lev Vygotzky's work, they state that rarely do schools allow room for more mature manifestations of play to develop—in which consciously representative or imaginary objects are used, more sophisticated imitative imaginary roles are played out, and produces themes in pretend play over a span of time. Though in this example play emphasizes the realm of pretend and imagination, it still highlights the potential to scaffold symbol, bodily and social engagement, with emotionally laden themes that would provide a foundation for adult creativity.

In the midst of conflicting views Piaget's sentiment about the interwoven developmental capacity for play is still useful. He stated that "imitation is a continuation of accommodation, play a continuation of assimilation, and intelligence a harmonious combination of the two" (1945, p. 112). Practically speaking, Piaget's "imitation" can be related to the social element in play which experiments with introjects (i.e., unconsciously enacted roles), while assimilation is the scaffolding of the physical play process itself. Intelligence, for Piaget, is the general capacity to bridge the developmental task of play (i.e., "being" for Winnicott)with social differentiation (Blom, 2004).

Physically, the psychomotor capabilities that are generated through the play process are also vital to holistic development (Mullan, 1984; Piaget, 1945; Trawick-Smith, 2014). This may not only be limited to the unfolding of visual-spatial skills and motor coordination, but the combinatory effect of combining such the increase in mastery of kinesthetic skills tied to emotional and social processes. Dance movement therapist Suzi Tortora (2014) explains that nonverbal experience can be emotionally evocative and integrative by bridging the connection between psyche and soma, as Winnicott

(1971) describes (Van der Kolk, 2014). While dance movement therapy may not be play in a traditional sense, the connection of emotionality with the pleasure of bodily movement and mastery, captures an adult version of developed expression, which childhood play might enable.

In fact, the relational forms of play (i.e., "peek-a-boo"), which begin in infancy, begin prior to overt symbolic play that occurs in toddlerhood with toys, games and developed motor skills (Fenson et al., 1976). Anthony Pellegrini (2013) hypothesizes that physical play using objects in social and peer contexts contributes to a stronger locus of social sharing of inventive and original ideas that emerge in play. The embodied, playful sharing of ideas and experimentation, could have implications for creativity, agency, and interpersonal processing later in life. In the recent publication *Wired to Create* (2015), authors Kaufman and Gregoire not only argue for the reclamation of this type of interactive and imaginative play for children to promote adult creativity; but draw upon research from researchers like Magnuson and Barnett (2013), to argue that playfulness actually enhances adults' well-being and ability to handle stress.

Together, the potential emotional, social and physical facets of play may buffer adult forms of creative expression. Granted, this has been empirically difficulty to locate and trace longitudinally (Bodrova et al., 2013; Lillard et al., 2013). But this does not mean a connection does not exist; but rather such connections may be so multi-dimensional that they are difficult to identify and measure across contexts and interpersonal setting. There are, however, studies that do support the integration of affect and cognitive experience, and physical experimentation in play (Bass et al., 2008; Russ, 2014). For example, play and reading have even been shown to strengthen childhood intellectual development, especially in low and middle-income countries (Maulik & Darmstadt, 2009). Such interventions may carry over longitudinally and cross-culturally, fostering greater emotional, physical, and social growth that can might give rise to a robust definition of creativity, just as Piaget (1954) and Winnicott (1971) have suggested.

Creativity and Play as Mutually Sharpening

Using Winnicott's understanding of primary creativity as the expression of an embodied self, freely exploring—play and creativity are not inherently separate processes, nor confined to childhood development. Rather, they are ongoing processes that sharpen each other and can inform clinical psychology. Sandra Russ (2013) draws on the work Bass and colleagues (2008) and Shaw and Runco (1994) to highlight that "fantasy and memory, experiencing emotion, cognitive integration of affect, and experiencing joy in creative expression," are essential to creative activity (p. 137). She concludes that such sweeping and complex definitions indicate that creativity may take a variety of expressed forms with the context of personality, work environment, and developmental context for skills. In light of this conclusion, Russ and Wallace (2013) contend that the developmental context which cultivates such a capacity is that of "pretend play" (p. 138). Pretend play weaves together cognitive and affective experience, which allows for the unfolding of the creative process.

Russ and Wallace (2013) offer a sound explanation of how formative experiences of play may scaffold the capacity for creativity by combining cognitive and affective dimensions of learning with bodily action. Russ and Wallace (2013) state:

> When children engage in pretend play, for example, we discover how they generate ideas and stories over a period of time. We can observe and measure their abilities to organize narratives: the amount of fantasy and make-believe in which they engage; their ability to symbolize or transform objects into representations of other objects (e.g., block becomes a milk bottle); their capacity for divergent thinking (i.e., to generate of a variety of ideas); and their skill at recombining objects, images, and story events. We can observe and measure their creative affective processes, such as their expressions of affect-laden themes and images (scary monsters, fighting soldiers, yummy birthday cake); their expressions of positive and negative emotion; their experiencing joy in playing and creating; and their integrating affect into a cognitive context (making affect fit the narrative). (p. 138)

An immersive simplification of this, is Winnicott's proposition that "being" precedes "doing"; and that it is from this place that original meaning is extended from a unique, developing self (1971). The sense of "being," or free exploration in psychic and physical safety, allows for pretend play—and the emergence of stories, symbols, experimentation, feelings, pleasure, and challenge to solidify within a person. The ability to "be" which allows for the integration of a sense of self rooted in discovery, can birth whatever "creativity" might look like for a particular individual. Optimally, pretend play prepares a child to integrate imagination and agency, yielding mature creative forms in adulthood, as described in the Tolkien reference above.

Whether this is formally in art, logic, or relationships: the creative journey is a person's own yearning to experiment and relate to the world as a unique agent. Creativity scholar Mark Runco emphasizes this as "personal creativity," which is universal, and marked by any intentional, discrete attempt to transform or to communicate something about their experience (2004, p. 23). Similarly, psychoanalyst Marion Milner held that the both play and artistic expression (i.e., creativity) mediate the tension of subjective experience into a more coherent emotional self-understanding. This happens when an intermediary form (canvas, paper, clay) is physically acted upon in a way that takes a part of their internal experience, desires or feelings that have not been integrated (or even dissociated) and locates them in an objective physical form. In both play and creativity, Psychic material becomes liberated in an external form which allows a natural reflection process to occur within a person (Milner, 1957). Just as Winnicott (1971) theorized, the acts of play that arise from genuine expression inherently contain personal meaning, that can be formulated into general creative output. This forms a natural sharpening between play and creativity, that can continue to grow.

VARIETIES OF CREATIVE EXPRESSION

What does it look like to access transitional phenomena within a potential space, across creative modalities? Though an extensive list could be detailed, it may be most helpful to reflect specifically on creative arts therapies that have already been studied in relationship to trauma treatment. By emphasizing the use of music, dance, poetry and visual arts therapies, the link between potential space and transitional phenomena will emerge as resources to not only facilitate recovery from trauma, but to consolidate new experiences that promote self-growth. Lusebrink and Hinz's ETC provides a framework for applying creative expression to trauma and growth, and indicates ways in which healing and growth might manifest through a variety of expressive art forms. Further, the connections that exist between creative modalities, trauma recovery, and personal growth all intersect in Winnicott's definition of the true self as the center of vitality for individuals.

Music, Dance, Drama, and the Visual Arts

Music, dance, writing, and the visual arts are all options that have been utilized and studied in respect to trauma treatment (Van der Kolk, 2014). They enliven the necessary movement between Herman's (1997) stages of remembrance/mourning and reconnection. Further they are all embodied forms of creativity that provide spontaneous opportunities for self-expression, akin to Winnicott's recommendations for eliciting transitional phenomena that can combine both conscious and unconscious content. Bessel van der Kolk (2014) explains "if trauma is encoded in heartbreaking and gut-wrenching sensations, then our first priority is to help people move out of fight-or-flight states, reorganize their perception of danger, and manage relationships" (p. 351). This is why he purports, especially in respect to children who have experienced trauma, maintaining an educational environment which includes "chorus, physical education, recess and anything else that involves movement, play, and other forms of joyful engagement" is so important. For adults, the need remains, though the form of movement, play and engagement may be more intricate. Van der Kolk reminds practitioners that the ability for music, dance and creative arts to "circumvent the speechlessness that comes with terror may be one reason they are used as trauma treatments in cultures around the world" (p. 245). In Winnicottian terms, such creative acts can help integrate deep affects of aggression and dependence, while bringing mobility to authentic personhood. Herman implicitly and explicitly indicates these processes during the remembrance and reconnection phases, which move back and forth for that trauma survivor (1997).

Music

It is difficult to delineate the origins of music therapy, as it has been utilized even in many cultures before literacy was developed (Bradt, 2006). But currently, even with the emergence of modern music therapy, the internal and external diversity of musical expression makes it a wide-ranging option for treatment. The American Music Therapy Association (2011) indicates the most popular modalities are African Drumming, Group Music Therapy, and Songwriting/Composition (LaVerdiere, 2006). Granted some of these expressions are more elaborate than others and require a higher baseline of proficiency, but the variety inherent in music lends itself as a multifaceted salve Empirically more specific evidence is still needed in respect to trauma recovery, but music therapy has a rich history in improving a variety of psychological difficulties (Garrido et al., 2015). One meta-analysis by Gold, Voracek, and Wigram (2004) has demonstrated significant main effects for music therapy treatment with adolescents experiencing a variety of psychopathology, specifically for behavioral and developmental benefit.

There are also several studies which suggest music therapy as an effective route to trauma treatment. Carr and colleagues (2011) demonstrated that individuals who participated in 10-week group music therapy significantly reduced PTSD symptoms, which they recommend especially for individuals who do not respond well to Cognitive Behavioral Therapy interventions. Another study by Bensimon, Amir, and Wolf (2012) demonstrated group music therapy to decrease intrusion of traumatic emotions, and increase the presence of non-traumatic emotions. Music therapy was even used widely in New York City by after the 9/11 terror to help individuals lower stress, cope more adaptively, and deal with traumatic effects. Interventions included a variety of skill levels—from improvisation, to singing, to practicing relaxation with music. Choir singing has even had powerful implications for improving heart-rate variability, and regulating breathing through communal synchronization . . . occurring through the vagus nerve, which has a role in regulation after trauma; (see Müller & Lindenberger, 2011; Porges, 2011). Psychoanalytic therapist and author Graham Music (2015) has even suggested that this evidence reifies Winnicott's emphasis on the psyche-soma connection, when it comes to the need for safety and holding in relationship to support creative action.

Winnicott held that culture itself could be a creative manifestation which provides then integrating function of psyche and soma, and music may be an ancient form which provides opportunity for the auditory exploration of the true self to grow (1954). Tying together aggressive percussive rhythm, sweet interdependent melodies of the cello, violin and guitar, or the mutually soaring and fragile nature of harmonic human voices forms a spacious realm for expression of pain, hope, tension and resolve. The complexity of dissonance and harmony, tempo, major/minor keys, modes and time signatures evoke sound that is connected to the body, and could yield new experiences of articulating a multiplicity of feelings. Transitional phenomena might emerge in the event that music can also be recorded, and then listened to by the individual so that they could tie their affect and narrate the experience in a new way. The transitional phenomena is the psychological and personal material embedded into the song; perhaps through lyrical grieving over a lost love, or instrumentally celebrating the sparks of a new romance through major chord swoons, or functioning to explore complex affects of excitement and trepidation associated with a particular life phase through nuanced rhythms and syncopation.

Dance

Intimately bound to the therapeutic potential of music, is that of movement. Expressive movement is also ancient, and dance is believed to be a universal occurrence in the history of human societies (Nemetz, 2006). Nemetz (2006) traces the history of dance in psychotherapy beginning with Classical Psychoanalysis, in which William Reich, building on Freud, hypothesized and observed that repressed feelings often where stored in the body through fixed positioning. She notes that this psychodynamic approach to repression and the body eventually intersected with the introduction of modern dance in the 1930s, and by the 1950s was catalogued as a mode of actualization from the perspective of the humanist therapies of Maslow and Rogers. By 1964, the American Dance Therapy Association was first organized. Dance/Movement therapy (DMT) has been suggested for treatment of eating disorders, the traumatic after-effects of sexual abuse, emotional pathology in children, and for individuals with sensory difficulties that have been conditioned after trauma (2006). DMT has been suggested to facilitate trauma recovery, and theoretically hypothesized to function to aid emotional regulation, by buffering the interoceptive sense which restores healthy physiological connection to one's body (Dieterich-Hartwell, 2017).

Levine and Land (2016) provided a meta-synthesized study of qualitative research concerning the use of DMT with trauma survivors. They found recurrent themes in the utility of DMT for trauma treatment which included—a restored connection between the mind and body, greater cognizance of the impact of trauma on the self through personal meaning-making, and infusing new patterns of relationship with various physical movements. From a Winnicottian perspective, the utility of DMT is an organic treatment option for a host of difficulties including developmental trauma. DMT is hypothesized to foster a sense of unity within the self, connecting "the psyche and soma . . . through a trusting play relationship" mirroring the maternal integrative function that "emphasizes the felt-experiential nature of dyadic play" (Tortora, 2014, p. 261). For Winnicott (1954), human beings are a born in psychosomatic unity, but the disintegrating effects of impingement form a gap between what we call the mind and the body. In the harmony of existence, the psyche-soma (i.e., mind and body) are in an irreducible relationship, unless, or until, trauma creates a separation between the mind and body (Van der Kolk, 2014.) Dance could even be an opportunity for re-union of the psych and soma, after the freezing and fleeing nature of trauma impedes safety, and stifles the ability for a spontaneous self to communicate. Granted that the pent-up grief, rage and longing involved in trauma may have difficulty finding expression through verbal narrative at first, bodily expression may restore the connection between psyche and soma while simultaneously giving relief to emotional pain storied in physical memory (Levine & Frederick, 1997; Van der Kolk, 2014; Winnicott, 1954). In a very similar way, the practice of yoga has also yielded benefits to individual well-being, and even trauma recovery, through promotion of the mind-body connection (Gard et al., 2014; Rhodes, 2015). Dance, like yoga, can become a practice of embodiment, a way to connect with the true self, and discover what emerges, providing a powerful outlet, especially in difficult times.

Poetry

While dance is a bodily communication of feeling, poetry may link thoughts with feelings, giving voice to the pain and longing the body carries. The psychic-somatic connection between writing and expression is also ancient, though only widely studied empirically for therapeutic benefit in the last few decades (Alschuler, 2006). The positive benefits of addressing emotional difficulties through expressive writing has been well-documented across three decades of research, and have even been shown to include mental and physical benefits alike in disclosure of trauma (Pennebaker, 1997, Pennebaker, 2000; Pennebaker et al., 1989; Pennebaker & Beall, 1986; Pennebaker & Chung, 2012). Poetry, is a special form of writing, in that the effort is also tied to novel communication which could have a robust idiosyncrasy and spontaneity typical of transitional phenomena. Poetry therapy (PT) is known to include fiction, autobiography, essays, short stories, journaling and traditional poetry as methods catered to the therapeutic needs of the individual (Alschuler, 2006). Alschuler described that PT focuses on "process" rather than "product" (p. 256), which, akin to

Pennebaker's conclusions, can help individuals working through traumatic distress shape a coherent story of trauma that can utilize "metaphor, symbol, and imagery" (p. 258) to reframe, understand, and communicate new meaning.

The use of metaphor, symbol, imagery in expressive writing can model an atmosphere of play. Playing with words, word meaning, syllables and combinatory phrasing is a linguistic atmosphere of "going-on being" (Winnicott, 1971). Going-on-being, for Winnicott, is simply the state of self in safety, spontaneity and exploration that occurs in an unhindered flow. According to Winnicott, extended time spent in a state of "going-on-being," also brings conscious, inner meaning in the process because it taps into the true self (1971). In regards to trauma, the creativity of poetry may even allow individuals who have difficulty narrating aspects of their trauma in mutually subtle, yet vivid forms, that could be hard to describe in a linear and systematic way. The use of poetry may allow an individual to capture the binaries of the chaotic pull between fight and flight, that may decathect specific words and identifications through a cohesive, yet intimate process. Like play therapy with the use of words, poetry might also elicit latent content, that could materialize into therapeutic transformation in the reflection process (Carroll, 2005). Binding together the particularity of poetic images with emotional struggle could be an opportunity to rediscover and reorient the true, deepest self in the midst of traumatic storms; planting a seed that dually releases pain of past events, while storying towards new hope.

Visual Arts

While less bodily driven than dance, and less linguistic than poetry, the aesthetic forms of creativity meets somewhere in between. The formal discipline of art therapy typically hones in on the use of visual arts for therapeutic intervention. Such art includes an array of visual content: painting, photography, drawing, and design with all their stylistic sub-genres.

While art therapy is still being established as an empirically supported therapy, it has yielded an entire subfield of trauma treatment in clinical practice that is growing as an effective treatment option (Avrahmi, 2006; Johnson, 1987; Johnson et al., 2009; Tripp, 2016). Treatment mediums range from conceptual to abstract art, realism to impressionism, the simplicity of graphic pointalism to the ethereal washes of watercolor, and the deep textures and hues of oil painting. All of these means create different emotional cadences for exploration—some sharper, some softer—some to be taken at face value, and some to be mined and narrated for hidden meaning. Much like the Rorschach the contents of creative visual art-making can bring to life unconscious meaning, frozen in the body that might even give a therapist insight into a client's process, if shared in session (Hass-Cohen & Findlay, 2015).

While establishing mastery in any visual art form takes considerable skill, learning to engage one's own personal meaning through exploration does not require mastery, though it might eventually yield mastery over time. Again, this is why Winnicott stressed that an artist can create a mesmerizing artistic product, without connecting real personal meaning to their process (1971). The healing potential of exploratory play with the visual arts relies on the individual's process—not the cultural ideal. However, in time it is likely that increased mastery and personal meaning may intersect as a medium of visual art is continually experimented with and used. In regards to trauma, it is absolutely essential that focus not over rely on structure, but on relational safety as structure, which anchors a freedom to express oneself. This is why Gant and Tripp (2016), art therapists who specialize in working with preverbal trauma, note that the initial foray into art therapy can require very basic, childlike ventures like "smearing" paint or chalk that is the beginning stage of removing the "mental shrapnel" (p. 69) of trauma, which lacks a sustained narrative. In Winnicott terms, such mental shrapnel are impediments to going on being, and their elicitation is part of the transitional experience that moves toward maturation (1953; 1965). Externalization of the shrapnel, the disintegrated affects and memories, moves to a blossoming into recovery—akin to Judith Herman's stage of reconnection, which will be described in the subsequent chapters (1997).

LUSEBRINK & HINZ'S EXPRESSIVE THERAPIES CONTINUUM (ETC; 2016)

In order to organize some modes of creativity, Lusebrink and Hinz (2016) have offered a framework for trauma treatment with the visual arts. Though this framework, known as the ETC, emphasizes the use of visual arts—the basic principles may also be theoretically adapted for the expressions of dance, music, and poetry. This could be accomplished by applying the ETC's method for individualizing trauma treatment in art to the concepts of maturation in Winnicott's theory.

The ETC proposes that art therapy can address trauma through the integration of three levels of creative experience. These include the Kinesthetic/Sensory, Perceptual/Affective, and Cognitive/Symbolic levels and can simultaneously offer a "top-down" or "bottom up" method to trauma treatment depending on an individual's needs and point in their own treatment. Kinesthetic/Sensory level includes the release of tension and physical energy (kinesthetic) while attending to color, texture, and spatial dimension of surfaces through touch. Examples of working with clay or hardware materials engage a primarily kinesthetic and sensory orientation. The Perceptual/Affective level includes the elements of color, line, shape that give boundary to form (perceptual), and the "increasing involvement with emotion, its expression, and the . . . affective . . . modification of forms" (p. 46). Formal artistic lessons on shape, line and hue can engage the perceptive qualities of this level, while acrylic painting or pastel can evoke higher emotional quality. Finally, the Cognitive/Symbolic level uses concepts, categorization, and creative problem solving (cognitive), as well as personal narrative and symbol (symbolic). Collage and sculpting are recommended at this level, as they involve stepwise progression with an element of narrative symbol that are common to such mediums.

According to Lusebrink and Hinz (2016), a bottom-up approach engages the sensory and kinesthetic elements first, before moving to the more symbolic levels of expression, where the emotional content of the creations are explored. Such an approach is common to psychodynamically informed play therapy, and is seems inherently Winnicottian in its beginning with spontaneity of the senses. The impulsive bodily interaction with media evokes primitive and complex feelings that can be represented through an act of agency that enables self-soothing, mirroring a mother's soothing within a holding environment, early in development.

A top-down approach would begin at the symbolic level—with an event like an intrusive daydream or nightmare. At this point clients are encouraged to re-imagine an alternative, desirable daydream or thought that represents the client an agent with strength and agency, rather than as a victim subdued by brutal or forceful circumstances, which can be affectively re-traumatizing. This creative process moves from the symbolic to the kinesthetic as emotions are reprocessed by channeling toward more physically interactive creativity. Though a top-down approach is less like an intervention Winnicott would use, the introduction of conscious contact with a transitional story is evident. It moves a passive, harmful fantasy, into actual creative engagement which provides contact with the true self (1971).

It is possible that the tenants of the ETC might actually relate to other dimensions of creativity mentioned above—namely music, dance and poetry. While dance harbors deep kinesthetic and affective components, music embraces cognitive and affective components, with kinesthetic movement being a secondary effect. Poetry often begins at a symbolic level of meaning, and moves to engage affect and senses through the use of words. Given a client's particular strengths and needs, this model could operationalize the creative need for transitional phenomena described by Winnicott (1953) to foster an adjunctive therapeutic experience. It offers a place to hold the emotional wreckage that lingers between sessions, without needing frequent contact with clients (Winnicott would often allow clients to visit at any point during office hours, which while noble, complicates the practicality of therapy for most therapists; Ulanov, 2005). Instead, through creative play, clients can negotiate their own transitional space to return to between sessions, given that the client has developed a network of safety that includes independent self-soothing practices for psychophysiological regulation, access to containing relationships, and an ability to identify potent triggers of hyperarousal.

Emergence of True Self toward a Theological Understanding of Creativity

Winnicott (1965; 1971) hypothesized that central to therapeutic movement is genuine creative expression. This even applies to recovery from trauma, by allowing fuller contact with the true self, which may have been sequestered due to the trauma. For Winnicott, religion (that is, the external "cultural" form of faith) was also, optimally, an extension of the true self searching for connection with God (Parker, 2011). Winnicott held that the discovery of self occurs through play, and that the centrality of this contact with the true, vital, and free core of a person is a lifelong journey (Winnicott, 1964). Returning to play is a way to nurture the self through a variety of ills. Stephen Parker stated that Winnicott's description of the true self, is not only psychological, but theological in that the "notion of a central, sacred core in humans is variously spoken of as the "soul" or "spirit" or the *imago dei* by theologians" (2011, p. 80). It is also of particular import that Winnicott's true self, the core of authentic creativity, is steeped in the influence of Wesleyan Methodist piety with its emphasis on Christ's love as the background to all real life, and its emphasis on freedom in the shaping human affection and love (Parker, 2011).

In discussing the origin of human personality, play, creative activity, love, and hope all have a relational foundation in psychology and theology. The theological ramifications of creativity extending from contact with the "true" self are multifaceted. In a way, though the Ancient Greek view of creativity as "muse" has been partially demystified through psychology, there is still an element of divine inspiration that may be true from a theological perspective. The difference however, is that creativity is not the realm of the genius, but it is mundane and accessible to everyone in their own way. Creative expression, designating an aspect of the *imago dei*, is also naturally a way to reclaim one's true identity as the "beloved" perhaps especially after worldview shattering events (Manning, 2009; Merton, 1961; Nouwen, 1979). The following chapter will more deeply explore theological perspectives that may enrich both a psychological understanding of play and creativity. This theological exploration will attempt to build cohesive theoretical connections between the *Genesis* narrative in scripture, the theology of play in the work of Jürgen Moltmann (1926–present), and the emergent themes that resound with an anthropology informed by both psychological developmental, and the impairment in wholeness that results from trauma. The healing potential of creativity, and its capacity to promote growth in the midst of trauma has some empirical, and much theoretical support in psychology; but also has theological support from the humanity as made in the image of God (i.e., anthropology), the work of the Holy Spirit (Pneumatology), and the hope of Christ's presence, work, resurrection and ascension (Christology). Creativity and play offer a grace and power that might bring fullness back to those who have been traumatized, and made to feel the corrosive impact of felt powerlessness and voiceless vulnerability.

3

Toward a Theological
Understanding of Creativity

STUDYING CREATIVITY HAS THE potential to bring insight, appreciation and humility towards what it means to be human. Yet, studying and discussing creativity still leaves much unspoken, and much unknown. With all of psychological theory, developmental research and neuroscience combined there is still a level of profound mystery involved in the meaning and extension of the creative process (Csikszentmihalyi, 1996). This, in part, is why faith may be so essential to approaching such mystery. Faith provides an invisible framework to the visible world, and can assist in binding the limits of human knowledge together from a posture of humility, gratitude, and stewardship. Faith can orient meaning-making, and so should not be dismissed as simply an "add on" to a psychological perspective (Park et al., 2017). Rather it is the transformative vision with which Christian's might interpret what scientific discovery offers. While the science of psychology has certainly exposed "shadows," wrongdoing and misinformation that has extended from various Christian faith traditions, isolating psychology and theology often only entrenches a false divide between disciplines, limiting our understanding of the world and constraining awareness of relationship with God (Bland & Strawn, 2014; Rohr, 2009). Instead, working towards a holistic integration between faith, science and psychology can provide the type of "resonance" between all of creation in a way that reflects the majesty of God's goodness in the world (Brown, 2004).

The previous chapter demonstrated various psychoanalytic and developmental perspectives of creativity, centering on the work of D. W. Winnicott and, reflecting on creative activities that have been used for recovery from traumatic experiences. This chapter, will move forward from a purely psychological perspective, and into an overarching domain of faith and meaning. The overall purpose of this current chapter is to integrate a theological perspective of creativity, which is grounded in the wider tradition of Christian faith. Given that the Christian faith holds so much internal theological diversity, this chapter is grounded in the limited field of the author's own resonance with sources from various theological traditions, which include Wesleyan, Franciscan (Roman Catholic), Eastern Orthodox, and global Charismatic/Pentecostal evangelical influences.

However, the hope of such a chapter is that it may still translate across Christian traditions, using the resources of scripture, theological reflection, and Christian integration in the field of psychology, to provide a robust movement toward a theological perspective of creativity. To accomplish a theologically integrative perspective of psychological development, that might respect all Protestant, Catholic, and Orthodox perspectives, the author will primarily use the work of theologian Jürgen Moltmann, but also utilize a variety of Old Testament scholars and Christian theologians broadly in the evangelical fold, respectfully referencing the Eastern Orthodox theology of aesthetics, as well as perspectives on spirituality offered by Franciscan monk, Richard Rohr. While Moltmann is the central academic source for this chapter, an integrative theological perspective may benefit from drawing upon, and respecting the input of scholars and authors of various theological traditions. In this way, this chapter hopes to operationalize some creative diligence by weaving together points using the richly colored fabric of global Christian traditions.

This chapter will begin with the "beginnings" in Christian scripture, exploring the book of Genesis and highlighting the creation narrative of Genesis 1 and 2, including the role of God's creative initiative, humanity as made in God's image, and the call to stewardship and flourishing in the earth. The theological and anthropological themes that emerge from this scripture will also be related to the psychoanalytic theory and clinical work of D. W. Winnicott, emphasizing creation out of chaos, the vitality of loving relationship as central to creative maturation, and the roles of stewardship, rest and play in promoting creative action. Next, this chapter will move from the themes discussed in Genesis 1 and 2 toward a theological investigation of play as a foundation of human creativity, drawing upon the work of Jürgen Moltmann (who while broadly located as a German Reformed theologian, has attempted to provide an ecumenically applicable trinitarian theological perspective; Moltmann, 1992.) This will build upon on the themes of vitality, awe and wonder, and liberation or "Easter freedom" (Moltmann et al., 1972) that can be recovered through play and creative expression. Finally, the role of play and creativity in the community of faith will be discussed in regards to working through the varieties of collective and individual trauma. This will emphasize the role of spirituality in both apophatic (deconstructive) and cataphatic (declarative) creative forms, and the move to connect the potential theological implications of Judith Herman's approach to "bearing witness" to trauma within the Christian community.

GENESIS 1 & 2

The biblical creation story provides a baseline for understanding God's relationship to and original intent for the world (Lamb, 2011). The narrative genre, and liturgical style of Genesis invites an intimate and communal depth that is simultaneously participatory and imaginative (Brueggemann, 1982; Goldingay, 2003). The themes and truths embedded in the book of Genesis are so deep, layered, embodied, earthy, spiritual, yet mystical in their comprehensibility that a purely modern and reductive "scientific" approach to such scripture may rob the story of its dimensionality and power. Truly, it is also the multiplicity of readers, and the presence of the Holy Spirit that continues to bring scripture alive, and orchestrate these stories into the broader reality of resurrection and salvation that God brings to a broken, distorted, shattered, hurting, and self-destructive world (Gonzales, 1996). Genesis, the "beginning," is a scripture that emerged in the midst of many similar, but competing narratives in the ancient Near East (ANE) including Egyptian and Mesopotamian myths. Many of the creation stories in the ANE, such as demonstrated in the Enuma Elish, portray similar patterns of creation, human formation out of the raw earthen material, fall/rebellion leading to strife, and even cataclysmic flood stories, as contained in Genesis (Brueggemann, 1982; Goldingay, 2003). However, the person of God presented in Hebrew scripture, and the corresponding place of and value of humanity and creation, is vastly different than neighboring mythologies. Though the patterns of the story are similar, the character of God (or gods for the ANE), and the value placed on human beings speak to a fundamentally different reality.

To summarize—and for the sake of brevity, oversimplify—in the ANE creation narratives, it is common for the gods to be portrayed as capricious and competing, while humans are portrayed as relatively undignified and striving in their origins (Lamb, personal communication via lecture, 2011; Sarna, 1989). The Genesis story, however portrays a deliberate, and singularly powerful God. The God of Israel is personal, and creates out of the void of nothingness, bestowing humanity with original dignity, purpose, agency, all in a context of full relational harmony with God's self and with all creation (Brueggemann, 1982; Sarna, 1989). The three thematic elements that will be investigated from this scriptural landscape for theological and psychological import are the roles of creation out of "formlessness," being made in the "image" of God, and the creative role of stewardship in the context of relationship. A rereading of scripture from an integrative psychological perspective may function as a small act of creative stewardship, intended to widen the lens of divine enchantment and fullness which God intended and extended for humanity from the beginning. These themes form an anthropological bridge to creativity from scripture, while extending the meaning of creativity in psychological development through theological resonance.

Creation out of the Formlessness

The book of Genesis details the origins of the earth and human beings with striking intimacy. Genesis chapter 1 illustrates such origins by beginning with God's presence in the midst of a dark, unformed space. God's presence then introduces something new by speaking the earth into life. The NRSV translates Gen 1:1–2, "In the beginning when God created the heavens and the earth, the earth was a formless void and darkness covered the face of the deep, while a wind from God swept over the face of the waters." God then creates, by speaking light into existence, calling it "good," and separating day from night. Next God continues to speak water and land into existence, vegetation, the "dome of the sky" (1:14), seasons, "swarms of living creatures" (1:20) in the air and the sea, and eventually all land-inhabiting animals. Each time God creates, God appears to reflect or declare on what has been made, calling it "good." Sarna (1989) elucidates that God's repetition of observing that creation is "good" "affirms the consummate perfection of

God's creation . . . [showing that] reality is imbued with God's goodness" (p. 7). The readers are invited into a world that began in formlessness, and by God's good will is filled with expansive and diverse creation.

Jewish scholar Nahum Sarna indicates that the Hebrew word for create, *bara'*, in this instance is spoken "exclusively of divine creativity . . . the product is absolutely novel and unexampled, and depends solely upon God" (1989, p. 5). It is a type of creativity that human beings cannot manifest. This initial creativity is also special, because it is something that begins with God's free giving (Brueggemann, 1982). Additionally, Sarna (1989) describes that the Hebrew language for "unformed" (or formless) "void" is *tohu vabovu* "designates the initial chaotic state of the earth" (p. 6). The scripture affirms that out of this chaos, God creatively and gracefully brings goodness through free action. The theological implications of starting the narrative this way are vast in reference to God's own creativity, and eventually, as the narrative proceeds, also endows human beings with their own creative potential within the context of God's creation. Being made in the very image of God, humanity is invited into the creative process not through their own earning, but by God's pleased intent. Though humans cannot create "out of nothing," their creative potential was gifted within the context of creation (Brueggemann, 1982). The divine image within humanity can surface to bring beauty, hope and a "new song" (Psalms 40:30, 96:1) to the earth.

Brueggemann argues that the actual historical context of Genesis was written by Israel in a state of exile (1982). Old Testament scholar John Goldingay (2003) goes as far to state that

> Israel was aware of the evidence that formlessness, darkness and tumult could characterize the world . . . [as] its own life descended into an empty void . . . The beginning of [Israel's] gospel assures us that this experience need not constitute God's last word, because it was not God's first. (p. 53)

Such theological implications are vast, but the psychological implications are an immediate parallel to the process of human development, including the development of creative capacities.

The state of formlessness mirrors the origins of human development; as infants begin in a state of utter dependence, and find life in symbiosis through their caretakers, being protected, nourished and even "spoken" into psychological life, before any true agency is available (Ulanov, 2005). Humanity's capacity to procreate physically, and imprint psychologically emerges from utter formlessness in the "void" of the womb. In the same way, human psychological development occurs through a blend of dependence and adversity. Like Israel, humanity's state of dependence eventually yields challenges and conflicts that lead to maturation. Facing the fears of individuation, and the harsh realities of the world, including trauma and global strife, might reflect inevitable experiences of exile towards the physical body, and even the "true self" as Winnicott describes (1971). Winnicott's vision of creative development occurs in the outside world, but begins from an inner spark, that requires the love of initial holding experiences in vulnerable, chaotic states of dependence (Mayo, 2009; Ulanov, 2005).

Psychoanalyst Marion Milner (1957) also emphasized a similar perspective on creativity, seeing that creativity originated in a "void," because creative action requires a process of letting go that begins in the state of accepted chaos. Acceptance of chaos, exile, and formlessness is actually the training ground for authentic creative experimentation for Milner. Mayo (2009) highlights that Milner's suggested state of chaos was a practiced release of the self, that allows for free association and integration, and even for spiritual growth. It could be said that Milner's process of letting go, is a primitive act of humility, that acknowledges the felt formlessness of dependence, and the grace of life that allows for and sustains creativity. The parallel between Milner's hypotheses towards the creative process is one that is regressive in an objective perspective, but in vulnerable regression allows the inner voice of the individual to arise in a deep and liberated way (Parker, 1996; Parker, 2011). From a scriptural perspective, this is the initial dependence on God's grace, not only to create, but even to exist and steward the created resources in the earth. The creative process of child-rearing, even in its pain and difficulties, mirrors the grace of God's gifting emerging in new life; just as the creative process of everyday life has been founded in an original blessing (Lamb, 2011).

Made in the Image of God

Blessing may be viewed as the original context of creation. Before the Genesis story introduces the fall of human beings and the introduction of sin, shame, and death in chapter 3, there is a poetic and sacred description of the unique place of human beings among the rest of creation, on the sixth day of creation. On the sixth day, God speaks humans into existence "Let us make humankind in our image, according to our likeness; and let them have dominion" (1:26) over all the living creatures in the air, sea and land. At this point there is a repeated phrase "So God created humankind in his image, in the image of God he created them; male and female he created them" (1:27). God then "blessed" them, and said "be fruitful and multiply, and fill the earth and subdue it." Genesis 1:28 narrates how God has given every plant and seed on the earth, and every tree and corresponding seed and fruit, and to "everything that has the breath of life, I have given every green plant for food" (1:30). However, this day is special. God declares it "very good" (1:31). Nahum Sarna (1989) states that the phrase "in our image, according to our likeness" is an intricate combination in Hebrew, that uses phrasing that is "virtually identical in meaning," and highlights the particularity of human nature and "their special relationship to God" (p. 12). This relationship is special in that only human beings are made in the image of God.

In fact, there is a stark contrast to ANE creation narratives here, as Egyptian and Mesopotamian narratives would only elevate kings or ruler of the land to likeness of the gods. The Genesis narrative, however, uses "regal" language towards all humanity; as "each person bears the stamp of royalty" (Sarna, 1989, p. 12). Although with this special endowment, humans are called to rule the animals, plants and land, the particular type of creative rule is in the image of a Creator who is gracious, and blesses creation with both powerful affirmation and tender care. The royalty of the human race bears semblance to a God who is vastly different than the neighboring narratives; there is no exploitation, power mongering, or carelessness. Instead, there is generosity, patience, kindness and intentionality. This theme is again illustrated in Gen 2:18–20, as God invites Adam to name the animals. Such an invitation demonstrates God's affirming, generous, and relational desire for humans to use their creative faculties to bless creation in a personal way. The invitation to name animals, again, manifests God's free, desiring, generosity. Animals are not the creation of human beings, and in all their goodness, are given to humans for ruling and naming. This interaction, which bestows royalty, fruitfulness, gracious ruling, and blessing to human beings sets a context for our intended creativity. This blessing also provides a personal creative mark to give to the animals. This activity does not engrave a sense of dominative ownership, but of companionship and stewardship (Sarna, 1989). Human beings are gifted with the ability to bear the creative likeness of their creator, in a very personal, collaborative manner, manifesting the image of God within. But creative activity is not the extent of fullness in the Genesis story. Rather, creative activity is finally connected and grounded, or consummated, in rest.

Stewardship, Rest, and Play

Genesis 2:1–3 begins:

> Thus the heavens and earth were finished, and all their multitude. And on the seventh day God finished the work he had done, and he rested on the seventh day from all the work he had done. So God blessed the seventh day and hallowed it, because on it God rested from all the work he had done in creation.

Walter Brueggemann (1982) states that Genesis "moves from . . . God's confrontation with chaos (1:2), to the serene and joyous rule of God over a universe able to rest" in the rest of the chapter (p. 22). Rest is introduced, not as a constraint to creativity, but as a gift, and a source of return to a sense of being that allows a remembrance of our loving connection and dependence on God, the original creator. Sarna indicates that "the seventh day is in polar contrast to the other six days, which are filled with creative activity. Its distinctive character is the desistance from labor and its infusion with blessing and sanctity" (1989, p. 14). Sarna also emphasizes that the human order of Sabbath or *shabbat* is not present in the narrative, as this was particular to Israel in their covenant with God. However, this story sets a universal context for the Sabbath, which is singular among neighboring creation stories. Not only is the Genesis narrative unique in God's creative, personal and loving power, but it also unique in that it is the only narrative to introduce the rhythm, modeling, and freedom of rest.

The readers of this portion of sacred text are invited to break creative action—and return to a place rest. Again, knowing that God is all powerful and certainly had no need to cease from creative activity, God still rests on the seventh day—as a gracious modeling (Johnston, 1983). In the New Testament Gospel of Mark, Jesus reminds his disciples that "The sabbath was made for man, not man for the Sabbath" (2:27). The theological implications are again vast, but the historical context of Israel may provide an immediate parallel for the humanity—acting as a microcosm of the human condition (Moltmann et al., 1972). Just as Goldingay's (2003) emphasizes that the book of Genesis was likely written in a state of exile, reader's may also be reminded of Israel's captivity in Egypt, and prophetic message of

Isaiah, stating "For thus said the Lord God, the Holy One of Israel: In returning and rest you shall be saved; in quietness and trust shall be your strength" (30:15 NRSV). Rest in return to relationship are the original, and continual call for human's restoration, sustenance, and hope.

Robert Johnston (1983) conveys that for the Hebrew people, Sabbath was not a day of cultic practices, as commonly understood in modern western Christianity. Instead it was a ceasing from work, and for which Johnston argues, is a parenthetical space for play and "refreshment" which "organizes" the rest of life (pp. 87–89). Johnston communicates that "for those who would become lost in the intoxication of creative work . . . the play of Sabbath is a reminder that we cannot ultimately find meaning by mastering life" (p. 92). There is rest in God's abundance and sovereignty in creation that seems to be primary relational: humans are meant to return to God's holding, which is psychic, physical, spiritual and ultimate (Moltmann, 2015). From this place humans can learn to savor God's creative work, and be renewed in their relationship and intentional, royal and loving place in creation (Brueggemann, 1982; Moltmann, 1992). This deep theological message might anchor human anthropology in God's gracious intent, and perhaps is what Winnicott (1954; 1965; 1971) mirrors in his own developmental theory, as he reminds readers that creativity is valued insofar that it is personally meaningfully (both existential and intimate), rather than "productive" in a modern economic sense.

Reflecting on the work of Winnicott, scholar Stephen E. Parker (2011), highlights that Winnicott's work introduced "art, play and religion" as means that "can move one toward greater integration of their personality" (p. 140). This is significant because art, play and religion emerge in, and as transitional space that "allows for the tapping of the creativity that belongs to play" (p. 140). For Winnicott, creativity that stems from play brings health, and is imitative of a type of psychological fullness that is simultaneously aggressive and dependent, unconscious and conscious, imaginative and communicative, bodily and spiritual (Ulanov, 2005).

Winnicott (1971) emphasizes that play requires a level of rest, which can be viewed as an acceptance of "unintegration," or "going on being," that brings contact with aspects of the true self, which may become mired by the pressure of productivity. The creation narrative of Genesis anchors theologically informed anthropology, bookending creative action with a return to rest, the joyfulness of play and the ultimate origins in a sovereign creator. Winnicott's hypothesis that creativity is distinguished in its foundation in playful being, is imbued with spiritual significance. Such a theory bears semblance to many of the themes illustrated in the Genesis narrative—including the gradual development of the dependent and chaotic psyche from an initial holding space; and the requirement of loving relationship as central to creativity and discovery.

Granted, the origins and intention for all creation takes a drastic turn in Genesis 3, when sin and death are introduced, distorting the harmony and full connection that permeated Adam and Eve's blessed place in the garden. But too often perhaps, theologians and psychologists alike, focus on the effects of pain, death and distortion before remembering the original role of God's gracious affection in shaping persons. Genesis portrays the initial freedom and wholeness of personhood, with a pivotal phrase "And the man and his wife were both naked, and were not ashamed" (2:25 NRSV). This phrase in and of itself may evoke a sense of rest, and fullness; and absence of self-consciousness and anxiety, and a presence of life-giving vulnerability and intimacy, that is unfiltered, reciprocal, and pure (Cooke, 2010). This picture may evoke a sense of the spontaneous, free and inherently playful and creative self like Winnicott attempted to access as the therapeutic energy of life (1953; 1965; 1971). But more so—it conveys the anthropological intent of a theological vision—that is the fullness of relational harmony with God and creation, in the context of gracious acceptance and "choseness" in being God's own creation (Moltmann et al., 1972).

The reader of the Genesis story is invited to reflect that before sin entered the world, humans were naked and had no shame. Richard Beck (2012) suggests that the introduction of shame and fear into the human psyche are primary disintegrating effects of sin and death; before which, there was no condemnation of self and others, self-conscious hindrance to connection to our bodies, or impediments in our ability to live in the wholeness, joy, and expressive communication with God and one another. The readers of Genesis might imagine that before sin, authentic creativity is grounded in the pleasure of rest, naturally exuded from our being.

If God is the source of our wholeness, and the ground from which we may even learn how to take pleasure in rest, our anthropology is inevitably impacted. If anthropology informs psychological theory, faith may also bring a restorative vision of anthropology to current perspectives in psychology (Shults & Sandage, 2006). Just as the parallels between the Genesis and other ANE creation stories illuminate palpably different worldviews, the theological meaning which extends from the Genesis narrative might empower Christians to think differently towards human potential and purpose terms of creativity, stewardship, and play. Instead of a worldview built on striving, competition and comparison, the Genesis narrative beckons God's desire for human beings to live in harmony, gratitude in work and play, and safety and freedom that comes with intimacy.

JÜRGEN MOLTMANN'S THEOLOGY OF PLAY

Genesis is only the beginning, perhaps, in both scripture as well as theological meaning making. Genesis offers powerful theological and anthropological anchors, which are enriched throughout the rest of the Bible. From a Trinitarian theological perspective, this also includes the role of Christology (the study of the person and work of Christ), and Pneumatology (the study of the person and work of the Holy Spirit) (Kärkkäinen, 2002; Kärkkäinen, 2016). A holistic Trinitarian theology of play should include anthropology, Christology, and pneumatology together, and there are few if any better resources to provide such a perspective than the work of theologian Jürgen Moltmann. Particularly, Moltmann's *The Spirit of Life* (1992) emphasizes creative vitality as originally empowered by the work of the Spirit in creation, while Moltmann's *Theology of Play* describes the pivotal importance of awe and wonder in Christian play, and the impact of the resurrection in renewing our creative, playful and aesthetic senses as a refuge and connection to joy (Moltmann et al., 1972). Together the theological points of vitality, awe and wonder, and renewal in "Easter freedom" all harness the importance of human experience in connection to God, which allows space for continued integration of psychological theory and practice.

Vitality and *The Spirit of Life* (1992)

Moltmann makes the point that often in the history of the Christian theology, God's Spirit and spirituality, have become distanced from everyday life through the influences of Gnosticism in the Augustinian tradition, which were largely impacted by Greek philosophy. Gnosticism regards created matter and spirit as opposing forces, which denigrates the physical vitality of creation, and elevates the immaterial (1992). Moltmann states that this perspective is not found in the Old Testament, and such a "spirituality introduces an antithesis which splits life into two, and quenches its vitality" (p. 84). Gnosticism is very different than what the readers of Genesis encounter, when God repeatedly calls creation "good" and human beings "very good" (1:31), emphasizing that a creative invitation to name the animals, to "fill the earth and subdue it" (1:28), and in their original state were "naked and unashamed" (2:25). Rather, in the Old Testament, as Moltmann eloquently states "God's Spirit is the life-force of created beings, and the living space in which they can grow and develop their potentialities. God's blessing does not quench vitality. It enhances it" (p. 84). The Old Testament, and created goodness of the world in Genesis might set such an important context for anthropology and theology of play, because it speaks of our original unfiltered attachment to God, and joyful pleasure taken in God's gracious gift of stewardship.

Moltmann (1992) continues:

> We do not find anything comparable in the New Testament or Christianity's original messianism either. There God's Spirit is the life-force of the resurrection which, starting from Easter, is poured out on all flesh in order to make it eternally alive. (p. 94)

This theological perspective beckons Christians to envision the work and immanence of Christ as something that was fulfilling what God desired for his creation since the beginning. It is a renewal, but also a raising of the dead into new life in which the Spirit "places the whole earthly and bodily person in the daybreak colors of the new earth" (p. 95). This might be interpreted as a new life, but also a new freedom which the Spirit brings to groaning creation, through the life, death and resurrection of Jesus. This theological hope is captured in Paul's epistle to the Romans in which he states such hope is

> that creation itself will be set free from its bondage and decay and will obtain the freedom of the glory of the children of God. We know that the whole creation has been groaning in labor pains until now; and not only the creation, but we ourselves who have the firstfruits of the Spirit, groan inwardly while we wait for adoption, the redemption of our bodies. (8:21–23)

This scripture not only reflects freedom from bondage and decay (which psychologically, clinicians might see developmentally in the many forms of trauma, impingement, abuse, organic illness and imbalance, isolation, and relational entropy), but it also reflects the hope of the Spirit towards a relational and holistic redemption and embrace through "adoption." While the human mind may not even be able to comprehend what this means in its fullness, it may an act of creative stewardship to try to imagine with God, what such freedom and wholeness might look like (Brueggemann, 2001). The child-like energy exuding from loving adoption, provides an ultimate sort of holding environment that Winnicott emphasizes, which is grounded in God's love. The vitalizing energy of adoption may bring with it a certain playful energy; and perhaps the type of spontaneity that Winnicott describes as the bodily expression of the true self (1971).

Moltmann draws upon the collective biblical witness to identify that the original experience with God was one "of an immense liberation—of being set free for life." This includes "Inwardly, their energies for living are freed from obstructions of guilt and the melancholy of death. Outwardly, their compulsions of economic, political and cultural repression are broken" (1992, p. 99). This statement might reconcile Winnicott's vision of the healing capacity of the spontaneous self, returning to a state of playful, unimipinged "being," that is ultimately grounded in loving connection, holding and safety (1965; 1971). In this way, the Spirit, might be the field of love that surrounds us, while human relationship is the opportunity to provide immanent empowerment of the loving connection that helps an individual access their genuine, liberated, and whole self. The freedom and life-giving energy of the Spirit of creation, released personally through Christ's work, might enable us to know a deeper level of play and rest, that is grounded in union and harmony.

The perspective of Moltmann (1992) emphasizes that in scripture, the experience of God and life-giving liberation are consonant and simultaneous. Our covenantal bond with God is also tied to the outworking of the Spirit of freedom, and the presence of Christ with us as Immanuel (Matt 1:22–23). This covenantal and immanent presence empowers vitality and freedom which resounds into all aspects of life, including our embodied psychological reality. In this way the vitalizing energy of play also has its source in God's presence before, beside, around, and within us (Moltmann et al., 1972; Sumsion & Alexander, 1985). It allows for true play, because we are safe and whole in our attachment to God through God's gracious seeking and outpouring. Creativity that stems from this foundation is life-giving, robust and energizing (Brueggemann, 2001; Moltmann, 1992). Further, this energy is ultimately grounded in the liberating, playful, and restful return to God's holding and the presence the Spirit which holds all of life together (just as manifest in Sabbath), without any of our own doing

(Johnston, 1983; Moltmann, 1992; Moltmann et al., 1972). Such energetic experiences of play may become symbolic acts of liberation, which help individuals tap into a sense of personal connection to God's presence eliciting moments of awe and wonder.

Awe and Wonder

Psychologically, the definition of awe has been described as an "emotion of perceived vastness" wherein "one is struck anew by the vastness, beauty and complexity of the surrounding world" (Danvers & Shiota, 2017, p. 938). Awe, theologically might also be described as experience of beholding something that transcends categorization and immerses an individual in gratitude, reverence, humility, and affection that is "revelatory"; in that it reveals God's nature which defies linguistic boxes and broadens our understanding of ourselves as God's creation (Johnston, 2014, p. 6). There appears to be an agreement between disciplines of theology and psychology about the basic experience of awe, as a powerful trajectory connecting the mind, body and emotions in a new extended experience. Stellar and colleagues (2017) found that exposure to expansive views of nature and corresponding awe to even elicit affective self-reports of humility. Danvers and Shiota (2017) discovered that experiences of awe significantly reduced the propensity for individuals to rely on internal scripts, when processing written narratives. What such results might suggest, is that the experience of awe can expand an individual's narrative and attention to the world; rather than reducing it to a previous filter—like a schema, internal working model, or unconscious projection.

Such experiences could transcend what individuals think they know about the world, and create new experiential connections between themselves, the world, and their experience of God. This, it seems, is the type of vitalizing and liberating experience Moltmann believes play can elicit and represent (1972). The freedom established through the Spirit's presence in play, and remembrance of the original purpose in God's creation, might bring an individual back into the joy of their "adoption" in Christ, and forward in their invitation to the new creation that they are becoming (Moltmann, 1992; Moltmann, 2015). This profound movement—returning and remembering we are God's own children, and adopted coheirs with Christ (Rom 8:17); while simultaneously embracing the indwelling Spirit, who is forming us as a new creation (2 Cor 5:17) engenders true play, the safety of our inheritance and belovedness, and the discovery of God's ongo-ing work in the world. God's work, inevitably, is a surprise; and it does not diminish the senses but sanctifies them in the glory of the coming kingdom (Moltmann, 1996; Smith, 2017; Wright, 2006). This idea is reminiscent of Winnicott's emphasis on the importance of moments in which patients surprise themselves in their spontaneous living (1971). Both in play and psychotherapy, this moment yields the benefit of reinforcing the energy of discovery, of the freshness and living nature of the environment. Moltmann indicates that spiritually transformative experience is not detached from the senses—but is experienced by a whole person—which makes it sensual (2015).

The sensuality found in the embodied play in the world might also provoke a sense of wonder. Wonder, as the sense of passionate curiosity, in-trigue, and openness to discovery has a history in the scientific and artistic breakthrough (Murray, 2016; Rothenberg, 2015; Sandelands, 2013). Amy Hollingsworth (2011) refers to this anticipation of discovery and creative investigation as "holy curiosity" (pp. 26–27). Moltmann et al. (1972) high-light that wonder, or "holy curiosity," is a sort of fresh awakening to God's creation in the wisdom of child-like experience. In this way, the act of play and posture towards wonder can "break the bonds of the immutable status quo" (p. 12) which stimulates openness to new ways of thinking and be-ing. The experience of wonder, encountered through play, may even prove a profound act of faith and courage in God's victory. A sense of wonder provokes a sense of discovery, that is reminiscent of spring—colors come to life, roots awaken, leaves bud, flowers blossom with new fragrance; the promise of new life begins to emerge from a potential desert of ice, snow and darkness. Similarly, play and wonder can harken the spring of our adoption, the rebirth of childlike wonder. Learning to play and cultivate wonder, might affect humanity's creative and renewed postured towards the world. For "The world turns into desert where the freedom of play has been lost" (Moltmann, 1972, p. 16). When the freedom of play is restored, awe and wonder can be cultivated.

Easter Freedom and Creative Expression

The celebration of Easter presents an opportunity to stand in such freedom, as "Easter joy is the earth's joy, too" (Moltmann, 2015, p. 92). Easter brings remembrance of the death and resurrection of Jesus, the conquering of the power of sin and death, and the ascension of Christ as victor over history. Moltmann contends that this victory realizes our freedom and beckons celebration, even in the midst of our pain and suffering. The act of play is not only a manifestation of our original created goodness, but also can be an eschatological proclamation. It is a celebration of Christ's victory on our behalf and God's gracious and powerful holding off all history. This type of resurrection freedom is not just something for the future, but might be embraced in the present, through playing in nature, basking in the sensual immersion of art and music, and spontaneous games of humor and sport. This type of playful immediacy is so apparent in children who are unhindered by the worries, tension and guilt of adult life. But Christ has provided confidence that he has conquered our guilt and fear, and consequently, has restored our authentic ability to play (Moltmann et al., 1972).

Winnicott's (1965; 1971) assertion that the loving dependence and discovery of early play is crucial to human development illustrates Moltmann's own emphasis on play, as founded in the gracious and abundant love of Easter. But Moltmann and colleagues (1972), and Winnicott together may even reflect a part of Jesus' own statement that "Truly I tell you, unless you change and become like children, you will never enter the kingdom of heaven" (Matt 18:3 NRSV). Of course, there are so many possible dimensions of understanding this statement, it is hard to overlook that this may very well be true to our psychological reality. The dependent, exploratory, playful and trusting posture of a child can teach adults about life in the kingdom of heaven. It may open up the eschatological truth of our liberation in Christ, so that we might be reborn into a new way of living. Moltmann et al. (1972) captures this eloquently in *Theology of Play*, stating:

> Faith is a new spontaneity and a light heart. In faith we accept ourselves as we are and gain new confidence in ourselves because we have been trusted more than we deserve and ever thought possible. The meaning of Easter lies in liberation from the compelling force of guilt and the compulsion to repeat evil. Easter opens up the boundary-crossing freedom to play the game of the new creation . . . The cross of Christ therefore does not belong to the game itself, but it makes possible the new game of freedom. He suffered that we may laugh again. He died that we may live as liberated human beings. He descended into the hell of the forsaken to open for us the heaven of freedom. He became a slave of the enslaved, a servant of those in servitude that these may become free lords of all things. (p. 32)

The promise, and freedom is visible and tangible in Christ's resurrection in which he returns to the disciples and even invites Thomas to touch his physical wounds (Luke 24:25). Christian therapists and clients alike might learn to trust as children in Christ's full conquering of death and sin, not by ignoring the wounds, but knowing that God restores all things and holds "the keys to death and Hades" (Rev 1:18). We might return to play as an act of liberation, and confidence that God has freed us.

If play is liberated, creative expression may be given a new foundation. Humanity's creativity no longer has the broken context of temporary survival, weighed down by the fear of death, but is freed as creativity held in the kingdom of heaven. Humanity is renewed towards in "free self-representation" as an "echo to the pleasure of God in his creation" (Moltmann et al., 1972, p. 21). Paul writes in Rom 12:2, "Do not be conformed to the pattern of this world, but be transformed by the renewing of your minds, so that you may discern what is the will of God—what is good and acceptable and perfect" (NRSV). One aspect of this transforming renewal, might actually occur by restoring our vision toward God's original intent and pleasure taken in creation; especially concerning our ability to see, and celebrate the image of God in one another.

Another aspect may also be learning to soak in the resurrection power by returning to the rest and holding of God, which might allow creativity to stem from a playful, authentic place of expression and joy, rather than a place of performance and constraint, which Winnicott describes as the false self (1965; 1971). Though the context of therapy may be a primer and a reflective environment to help build this capacity, there may be a fundamental need for wider communities that practice and live purposefully from a place of spontaneous expression. Especially given the variety of ways in which developmental, acute, and biological illness and trauma can hamper self-expression, finding an empowering, trauma-informed community can be essential for many individuals in learning to access their playful, spontaneous selves which have been lost, forgotten, or impeded by suffering and weariness.

CREATIVITY, COMMUNITY, AND TRAUMA

Theologically, the image of God is unique within and upon each person in respect to their experience, body, spontaneous energy, and personality. But the particularity of human beings is also highlighted by, and connected to plurality (Balswick et al., 2005). The image of God is present in the Body of Christ, which includes the immense personal, local, cultural and tradition-based diversity of the universal church (Hoekema, 1986). Psychologically, the formation of the self requires attuned relationship in order to help integrate both dependence and autonomy as non-exclusive elements of being (Mitchell & Black, 1995). Integratively, this might direct attention towards the role of the community in promoting play, creativity and self-expression towards the formation of people as whole, incredibly particular, yet inextricably relational creatures. Readers may also be very aware that the image of God is marred by sin, death and fear within the institution of Christianity in the same way as the rest of humanity. However, the promise of the Holy Spirit brings the possibility of reconnection to our "true" selves in community in the present, in spite of the distortion of death and sin. The Spirit released through Christ's work, now works within God's people, both individually and corporately. Ephesians 1:13–14 describes "In him (Christ) you also . . . were marked with the seal of the promised Holy Spirit; this is the pledge of our inheritance toward redemption as God's own people, to the praise of his glory" (NRSV).

Given that most of the early church had experienced profound perse-cution even to torture, imprisonment and death, and began as a marginal group of believers, this promise bears a powerful message towards Chris-tian hope and meaning (Gonzales, 2010). Moltmann (1992) connects the context of persecution and suffering, still to the importance of play and our creative potential in community by the power of the Spirit. He states:

> Easter freedom does not permit us to escape from the world or to forget about it. Rather it leads us critically to accept the world situ-ation with its unacceptable moments and patiently to bring about change in the world so that it may become a place of freedom for (humanity). Thus, both the laughter of Easter and the sorrow of the cross are alive in liberated (people). (p. 32)

Recovering the ability to truly play, and express individuality within com-munity through creative action may be spiritually charged to awaken the reality and promise of God's victory. But this does not denote that the com-munity ignores all the ills that constrain our ability to play. Just as Moltmann describes, learning to play in freedom is not accomplished by ignoring the brokenness and pain of the world, but by accepting it, in the knowledge of God's desire and power on our behalf. Such a theological perspective em-braces the potential even for creativity to stem from experiences of trauma.

Not because trauma is in any way good, but that God's image persists even in the midst of trauma, and the inheritance of Christ promises that the love of God may work towards good, even in tremendous adversity, and even in spite of the present evil of the age (Josh 1:9–10; Rom 8:28; Gal 1:4; Jones, 2010).

Judith Herman offers a model to help facilitate the practical, bodily, and incarnate aspects in recovering the ability to play and empowering the creative process, in the acute and long-term effects of suffering imposed by trauma (1997). Each aspect of recovery can involve the community, and serves to educate the public on the process of dealing with trauma. She first emphasizes the role of safety—which is both physical and psychological. The second stage, is remembrance and mourning, which facilitates the metabolic nature of processing traumatic memory and experience to remove the emotional and physical toxicity of trauma, and reconnection, which buffers the reconstructive and empowering elements of recovery into new life. Serene Jones (2010) suggests that mourning (or remembrance) is necessary to learn to move to a state of "wonder" which for her, means to "behold" the goodness of God's creation in the atmosphere of a fractured world (p. 163).

While psychoeducation for trauma may help inform and sustain an empathic, wise and patient holding space for victims in a community of faith, the maintenance of such a therapeutic environment could also foster moments of creative play that awaken agency and dignity. Creative expression provides a venue to express narrative and bodily elements of grief, aggression and confusion; the presence of community to hold this narrative prevents isolation, and might elicit empathic resonance between a variety of individuals (Hass-Cohen & Findlay, 2015). However, the additional layer that the community of faith can provide, is the encouragement, understanding and comfort in a hope for one another that is spiritually empowered in relationship to God.

The community of faith might serve as an initial network of safety in solidarity, and also container for the stage of grief and mourning through prayer and compassion. As individuals process trauma in the course of psychological treatment, establishing additional holding environments (Winnicott, 1971) is crucial to re-scaffolding a sense of safety, and a place for grief/mourning as described by Herman (1997). However, this context also builds toward Herman's final stage of reconnection. Hope is present during new experiences of psychological holding in a faith community, in drawing upon a hope in God that is stronger than the limitations of one's current psychological and physical circumstances. Dually, such hope can also emerge in personal recovery through expressed creativity within this same community. The creative process which is affirmed and empowered through hope in a God who is fully present with and among the people, provides a particular space in which spirituality and creativity may speak into a space that has become frozen and wounded by traumatic experiences. The intersection of spirituality, trauma and creativity in a faith community might provide a strengthened network for navigating such trauma, while simultaneously emphasizing an individual's agency and profound dignity.

Apophatic and Cataphatic Expression

So what forms might creative expression actually take in a faith community? Two broader paths for creative empowerment in the faith community may include apophatic (deconstructive, or negative), and cataphatic (constructive, or affirmative) approaches. The apophatic tradition has traditionally been characterized as a path of silence and darkness, while the cataphatic has been characterized by revelation and the conscious embrace of God's attributes, often demonstrating as the visible and audible form of external praise and worship seen in Christian traditions (Pentiuc, 2014; Rohr, 2003). Theologically, deconstructive (apophatic) and constructive (cataphatic) approaches may also intersect with the stages of remembrance and mourning, and reconnection within Herman's model (1997). What holds both routes of expression together within the faith community, is the powerful bond of loving union with God.

The experience of union maintains a mystical element that is both hard to predict, describe, and force; it is simultaneously transcendent and incarnate; differentiated yet immersive (Parker, 1996; Watson, 2003). In assessing and wondering about mystical experiences in the church (in this case, particular to the Pentecostal church), Stephen Parker (1996) notes that a traditional psychoanalytic vision may prematurely dismiss the authenticity of mystical union, as "pathological regression" (p. 117). Parker refers to the experience of mystical union in which the selfhood is not lost, but "found" as "creative regression" (p. 119). Creative regression is adaptive in nature, and serves to promote, rather than hinder psychological formation.

Parker concludes that the experience of speaking in tongues, or expressive immersion during worship, can actually facilitate a connection to a primal bond with God, rather than just reflect a manifestation of maladaptive regression in a specific cultural context, as traditional psychoanalytic perspectives might suggest. Regression (in the sense of letting go; of conscious striving and modulation, silence and mystical liminality is central to apophatic prayer, and the process of deconstruction. But often, the balances of everyday life require cataphatic affirmations—boundaries that create safety through conscious remembrance of God, such as verbal and intentionally constructive liturgy, songs and prayers. Both apophatic and cataphatic trajectories of prayer mirror similar directions of creative expression, that may provide a variety way to "bear witness" in the safe confines of a loving community.

Traditionally, the apophatic approach is a mode of prayer likened to the path of "descent" in which an individual moves into a mystical silence, and has trajectory toward the dark, mysterious birthing place of transformation that presents as chaos, "the desert" experience of wandering, or being in the "belly of the whale" as described in the book of Jonah (Rohr, 2003; Rohr, 2008). Apophatic spirituality emphasizes the "overwhelming," "incomprehensible" nature of God that transcends human understanding (Louth, 2012, p. 138). It is likely that individuals confronted with varieties of trauma, persecution and strife may need to be met experientially in a place that can reconcile, and dually hold, the overwhelming, incomprehensible aspects of suffering; allowing that space of descent, chaos, and wandering to unfold in its own time. An apophatic approach in scripture as Paul states that the "Spirit helps us in our weakness; for we do not know how to pray as we ought, but that very Spirit intercedes with sighs too deep for words" (Rom 8:26 NRSV). Bodily and emotional processing of trauma may manifest as screams, night terrors, a pleading for motivation to keep going, struggle with apathy, and rage; portraying moments that can truly become too deep for words (Van der Kolk, 2014).

The reality of pain cannot be dismissed, ignored, or dissociated if individuals are to encounter recovery; but the pain must be seen, heard and felt honestly (Herman, 1997); and a context of gracious holding, and received prayer, often demonstrated by the laying on of hands in the congregation, may be the most powerful form of unity. During a period of life when an individual's ability to pray in words ceases, and the "wilderness" is encountered, this time may also open up the opportunity for creative and prayerful intercession. Allowing creative space to both regress and communicate in a liminal stage may allow a narrative to unfold and psychological integration to occur (Parker, 1996). Creative forms of regression are places where play naturally occurs, but such play may also elicit the most primitive dependent and aggressive affects like fear, sadness, affection, and desire can be released, held, contained, and integrated (Ulanov, 2005; Winnicott, 1971). The deconstructive, liminal, apophatic "path of descent" may emotionally feel like an experience of "losing" the self, but the result of going through this journey can result in an honest, vulnerable, and intimate discovery of facets the true self (Merton, 1961; Milner, 1957; Rohr, 2003; Winnicott, 1971).

Psychologically, the apophatic can be likened to deconstructive, liminal and unconscious aspects of the creative process, in which the primary task is "letting go," simply being, and moving from a place that is guttural, preverbal and nascent. Apophatic expression may be likened the role of mourning in Herman's (1997) model; in which the experience of darkness, silence and unknowing is often the vast experience of confronting a trauma, after a degree of safety has been stabilized. The mourning process, involves remembering pain that may be impossible to logically understand. In this way, Herman's emphasis mourning might be linked to apophatic spirituality, in that it feels like the place of disorganization and fear, where a trauma is faced. Creatively this experience might tap into the processes Hass-Cohen and Findlay (2015) describe in scribble drawing, decalomania, and ink blot tasks, that can use a place of chaos to access the depths of the unconscious, perhaps a place where prayer may be most needed. Allowing the creative liminality that Hass-Cohen (2013) describes in creative abstraction tasks, can use the chaotic places of pain to generate visceral movement, offering them up in prayer to a God who promises a presence which we cannot escape, even "'If I say surely the darkness shall cover me, and the light around me become night,' even the darkness is not dark to you" (Ps 139:11–12 NRSV). It is perhaps in those spaces of liminality and darkness (similar to the earth in Genesis' creation narrative), that individuals can learn to let go of social or historic constraint, and begin to allow their own spontaneous movement, feeling and longing to surface, even in what feels like chaos and "formlessness" (Sarna, 1989).

However, once the deep well of apophatic grief, waiting and longing is given space to gestate, the natural movement may be towards concrete expression, overt symbol and narrative in the cataphatic process. This could represent Herman's stage of remembrance—and in the movement towards the stage of reconnection (1997). Visual, vocal, or written forms of remembering a trauma in a more concrete way might link an individual to a complementary need to embrace a cataphatic prayers and affirmations of worthiness and love. While cataphatic prayer has been likened to the "mountaintop" moments or periods where revelation is experienced, and celebration or overt praise is shared (Rohr, 2003), the cataphatic process might be linked to the overt, reconstructive process of narrative and belonging. Cataphatic expression even connect as moments of insight, or clarity about one's affirmed identity as a child of God.

Theologically the cataphatic has traditionally been used to describe the virtues and qualities of God (i.e., steadfast, all-knowing, just, merciful), as is common in systematic theology (Pentiuc, 2014; Rohr, 2003). In the creative process, this could be viewed as the conscious edge in art-making that yields clarity in the outgrowth of the healing process. This may even help consolidate experiences of revelation towards one's own creative potential, even in the midst of such life-threatening situations. Here, a creative work may be realized, and finished as a more conscious symbol. This is reminiscent iconography of the Eastern Orthodox tradition, architecture in the Roman Catholic church, and praise/worship music in Protestantism (Pentiuc, 2014). The narrative and intentionality in the cataphatic process is much more overt. But too often, perhaps, the institutions within the church attempt to skip over the apophatic process in times of intense pain, rather than allowing space for an apophatic journey to naturally yield a cataphatic moment.

Creatively, in both apophatic and cataphatic prayer and creativity in faith-based contexts, the hope is that even in the darkest of times there will eventually come moments of resurrection: glimmers of light that break through the darkness; moments of spontaneous, liberation, awe, wonder, and playful emergence that occur and rekindle a connection to a self-uninterrupted by trauma, and embraced fully in spite of it. Perhaps this is the most powerful testimony of God's sovereign embrace, as it occurs not when it is easy to entertain a grateful and open posture; but when we are unable to do so. Perhaps God's full, just, humble and powerful love might break through the tragedy and evil of the world in moments of play, surrender, relational meeting, mystical encounters, or some combination of all such moments. Through the process of recovery, it is possible that individuals may contact the compassionate, powerful and sustaining salve of God's embrace (Watson, 2003).

Connecting with such a sense of being loved uniquely and wholly, in the creative and meaning-making process might prime the capacity to play in joy, rather than escape. Just as Moltmann states, "Joy in one's own existence awakens in the experience of being loved" (1992, p. 280). If individuals are able to encounter safety, remembrance and reconnection in love, then trauma, pain, disintegration and injustice may be healed in a variety of ways (Herman, 1997). Jungian analyst and scholar Ann Ulanov (2005) suggests that when the personal and corporate body of Christ feels the intensity of abandonment, and our hope, imagination, and capacity for faith eludes us:

> A God we cannot imagine crosses the gap to us. Neither a subjective-object God—one of our personal or group images for God—nor an objective-object God—an image given us by religious tradition—this Other stands forth as its own object . . . We do not recognize the God who survives destruction and comes to greet us. We do not know this God's name. We do not know that this is the same God going on being, despite life's destructiveness even unto death, until this God gives us the power to recognize him as he recognizes us, by name. The One who was gone, has come. The One who was lost, finds us. (pp. 141–42)

Just as Ulanov describes, neither clinicians, the church, nor those who have experienced trauma may be able to predict the ways that God can break through, whether in a singular moment, or in a slow and intricate process. But what victims of trauma, clinicians, and the community may all participate in, is an intentional opening and affirmation of human dignity, and an expectation and confidence that God's love desires our restoration, healing, and union. This posture reminds the entire network of care what God has done, is doing, and will do in the in-breaking of the Kingdom that makes "all things new" (Rev 21:5 NRSV).

4

Clinical Applications toward Posttraumatic Growth

EXPERIENCES OF TRAUMA CAN shake the foundation of a person's self-concept, relationships and daily functioning (Cozolino, 2010; Herman, 1997; Van der Kolk, 2014). The helplessness, panic, disorientation, and insidious upheaval of trauma has been self-evident across time and culture, since before diagnostic criteria was developed (Herman, 1997). Theologically, Christian clinicians and clients may also face the historic, present and eschatological implications of the varieties and generations of trauma that persist in the world. Murder, rape, physical and sexual abuse, cultural and ethnic marginalization, enslavement, natural disasters, intergenerational patterns of dysfunction and emotional abuse, famine, war and political injustice are realities of a sinful and fractured world; and as discussed previously in chapter three, were not God's intention for a good and beloved creation, as described in the Genesis narrative (Brueggemann, 1982).

While the origin of sin and suffering from a theological perspective is beyond the scope of this current work, the fallout of sin and suffering, and the consequent desire for restoring, redeeming, healing and transforming the effects of sin and suffering are at the center of this investigation. In order to allow continuity for clinical and theological discourse, Judith Herman offers a broad yet particular definition of trauma in her seminal work *Trauma and Recovery* (1997). She describes psychological trauma primarily as an affliction of the powerless. During traumatic events, a victim experiences the helplessness of a force beyond their control, which can include natural disasters, war, famine, and tragic accidents; but may also include and be exacerbated by traumatic force within a social institution, family structure, or life cycle. The result is typically tragic for one, or more people. In each of these instances, a traumatic encounter incites a physiological and emotional stress response that exceeds an individual's capacity to self-regulate and maintain a sense of coherence and connectivity to themselves, and the world around them.

Though vast empirical and conceptual attention has been given to trauma treatment in the last several decades, clinical understandings of experiencing growth after trauma are relatively nascent (Calhoun & Tedeschi, 2006; Calhoun & Tedeschi, 2013). PTG is the possibility for an experience of new, positive growth that can emerge after traumatic exposure (Tedeschi & Calhoun, 1995). While there is still some debate as to whether self-reports of growth are face-valid for all individuals that confirm it, many individuals have reported experiencing significant, positive reorganization in particular areas of life, after highly disorganizing traumatic events (Linley & Joseph, 2004; Maercker & Zoellner, 2004). The conceptualization and measurement of such a pivotal experience may be imperfect, but it might also offer profound clinical, and theologically integrative possibilities. These theological possibilities are reflected by Moltmann's (1992) and Ulanov's (2005) similar description of a God who crosses our own concepts to meet us creatively and powerfully, even in suffering, confusion and loss. The theological effect of God's immanence, holding together the fabric of creation, and the Spirit's empowering presence, poured out on Pentecost even further orient the Christian's understanding and awareness of PTG; especially because spirituality and meaning making play formative roles in the emergence of PTG (Park et al., 2017; Yong, 2010).

In the second chapter an overview of the developmental effects of creativity were provided, emphasizing the work of Winnicott and the crucial power of holding environments that facilitate experiences of play, as well as the transitional experiences which occur during the act of play. The developmental capacity and rudiments of creative processes which begin with play, were then related to the process of trauma recovery and hypothesized as a contributing element of growth after trauma. In the third chapter these main points were connected to theological themes of God being the source of creativity, as described in the Genesis 1–3, and humanity's special place in creation as being made in God's very image. This also included a theoretical integration of Winnicott's work focusing on the importance of creation in places of chaos, and the essentially dependent need for love to scaffold creative maturity. This chapter also examined the work of theologian Jürgen Moltmann, to reflect upon the Holy Spirit's empowerment and the freedom of Christ brought to us through his life, death and resurrection. These themes were extended to practical acts of creativity that allow for moments of "bearing witness" to trauma in the church and world. Now, the aim of the current chapter is to apply the integrative psychological and theological understanding of creativity towards the possibility of growth after trauma, represented in the construct of PTG, attending to both the specificity and generalizability of this construct for clinical and subclinical populations.

However, in order to better understand the potential for creativity to expand the possibilities for PTG in the after effects of trauma, it is necessary to first reflect upon the wider context of trauma studies. For this reason, the current chapter will begin by exploring PTG in relationship to posttraumatic stress. Next, the current chapter will detail the neurophysiological resonance between creativity, trauma and the arts in order to establish empirical links to the process of trauma treatment, and the emergence of bodily and affective integration that can occur through moments of spontaneous communication and even play, as described in Winnicott's theory (1965; 1971).

Finally, this chapter will argue that the hypothesized mechanisms of change involved in the occurrence and promotion of PTG might be strengthened through artistic exploration and creative play. This hypothesis is clarified in the relationship between current research regarding PTG, the clinical applications suggested by Calhoun and Tedeschi (2013), and the theory of developmental integration through experiences of play suggested by Winnicott. Together, the utility of PTG within the field of trauma studies, the neurophysiological overlap between the expressive arts and trauma treatment, and the underlying mechanisms of change in PTG parallel the creative process in a way that invites new clinical opportunities and theoretical understanding.

POSTTRAUMATIC STRESS AND POSTTRAUMATIC GROWTH

If clinicians are utilizing creativity as a resource to expand the potential for PTG, diligent attention must be given to the development and location of

PTG within the wider field of trauma literature. This will be accomplished first by defining trauma and PTSD, and then describing PTG specifically in context of Judith Herman's framework of safety, remembrance and reconnection (1997). Furthermore, the five measured domains of growth included in the construct of PTG will be described to demonstrate how PTG might be observed in various aspects of person's life. Together these subpoints will help locate PTG within a cohesive scientific context of trauma studies, while emphasizing the emergent possibilities that PTG brings to the field.

Trauma and PTSD

In Herman's description, trauma is an experience that overwhelms and impedes a person's functioning within, and approach to the world (1997). In the language of behavioral-response, a traumatic incident introduces an acute or prolonged fear response which continues to manifest that fear intrusively, disrupting the natural rhythms of a person's life. The psychological markers of trauma include hyperarousal (the body's fight or flight priming, that results in physiological preparation to fend off a perceived threat), intrusions (a fearful re-experiencing, such as a flashback, that forces its way into conscious experience), and avoidance (attempts to escape from a perceived stressor by way of repressed or denied feeling, compulsive behaviors/thinking, and even dissociated affect and memory) (Cozolino, 2010). Additionally, the updated DSM-5 notes that trauma often includes distorted/negative mood and thoughts, which pervade a person's daily functioning (American Psychiatric Association, 2013). The result of trauma is essentially ongoing, and replayed, physical, mental and emotional experiences of fear, suffering, and disorganization.

For adults, when such symptoms persist after an acute trauma for more than one month, they meet criteria for the diagnosis of PTSD (American Psychiatric Association, 2013). It has been estimated in US studies that between 69% (Norris, 1992) and 72% (Elliott, 1997) of individuals will report a trauma at some point in their life but the prevalence PTSD is only estimated at 7.8% (Kessler et al., 1995). So, it stands to reason that many individuals who experience trauma, do not experience PTSD. Still, this does not equate to an absence of traumatic complications for the majority of the public who will experience a trauma: but rather suggests that most people simply do not develop the full diagnosable criteria of symptoms, which can be categorized as PTSD. The prevalence of trauma that exists at subclinical and subdiagnostic levels, reflects the importance of trauma as a general concern for practitioners of psychotherapy. Best practice, and public health may benefit greatly from an operationalized perspective on both healing and growth after trauma for those not meeting full diagnostic criteria.

Furthermore, the varieties of trauma can elicit different levels of likelihood for psychological diagnosis and comorbidity, suggesting the need for a nuanced understanding for the predictive individual, contextual and cultural factors that are implicated in trauma (Wanklyn et al., 2016). Posttraumatic stress, or the level of psychological impact and consequent symptoms that occur after a traumatic incident, can impact a person in various aspects of daily living. In examining the commonality etiologies of posttraumatic stress Joseph Briere (2004) lists a host of experiences known to cause posttraumatic reactions. These include natural disasters (floods, earthquakes, hurricanes), motor vehicle and transportation accidents, violence occurring between individuals (abuse, assault, rape, intimate partner violence, stalking), larger incidents of public violence (terror attacks, mass shootings), combat violence (war, police actions, prisoner-of war situations), sexual exploitation (sex-trafficking and prostitution), life threatening illnesses or physical injury, and vicarious trauma experienced through aid and emergency work (Briere, 2004).

In addition, individuals who have experienced child abuse or physical assaults as children are significantly more likely to develop PTSD, further complicating the clinical and subclinical predispositions and manifestations of traumatic exposure (Breslau et al., 1999; Kessler et al., 1999; Zaidi & Foy, 1994). Though this list could certainly become more expansive and specific, each person's individual response is hard to predict, and may include a presentation of multiple psychological difficulties. The possibilities of subclinical, delayed onset, and complex PTSD contribute to intricacies of trauma diagnosis, impact and responses between individuals, depending on personality and psychological history. Herman (1997) even notes that, "disguised presentations are common in complex [PTSD] and may initially present with physical or psychosomatic symptoms, "chronic anxiety or insomnia ... intractable depression ... or problematic relationships" (p. 157). Even though the ways in which clinical and subclinical trauma manifest between different individuals may be hard to predict, the potential negative impact may still be evident even through additional diagnostic criteria.

For example, it has been suggested that almost half of all individuals diagnosed with PTSD also reach clinical diagnostic criteria for Major Depressive Disorder (MDD; Rytwinski et al., 2013). In addition, individuals who report traumatic exposure have also been shown to experience almost 3 times the likelihood of functional somatic syndromes (Afari et al., 2014). Functional somatic syndromes are often difficult to understand in terms of origin, and include disorders like fibromyalgia, chronic fatigue, irritable bowel syndrome, variants of chronic pain disorders and temporomandibular disorder. Functional somatic syndromes lack full medical understanding, and are hypothesized to be potential psychosomatic bearers of stress substance use disorders (SUDs) and PTSD have also been shown to occur together frequently (Brady et al., 2004; McCauley et al., 2012; Ouimette et al., 1998), and even an individual reporting of subclinical interpersonal trauma has shown a significantly greater likelihood of developing an SUD (Thege et al., 2017). Yarvis and Schiess (2009) report that, even subthreshold PTSD have been shown to be predictive of significantly increased depression, substance use and health difficulties in veterans. Such studies reflect the prognostic and individual complexity of individual trauma responses. These studies also indicate the possible role of subclinical trauma in predisposing the development of various mental health concerns.

This reifies the hypothesis that trauma may become stored in the body, and become entrenched in a way that disrupts emotional regulation and physiological functioning, negatively impacting one's ability to cope, connect with others, and with one's self (Van der Kolk, 2014). Given the large proportion of the population that will be exposed to trauma over a lifetime, and the implicated risks for developing PTSD and other psychological disorders, the effects of posttraumatic stress may systemically permeate society at a number of levels; making psychoeducation and availability of treatment critical for many individuals and organizations (Breslau et al., 1999; Kessler et al., 1999). At the same time, this may also suggest that the construct of PTG and the possibility for new positive growth is also applicable to the public. If there is a genuine occurrence of PTG in some individuals who experience trauma, being able to recognize this growth as one aspect of recovery and treatment might have broad systemic ramifications for clinical and public benefit.

PTG and Herman's (1997) Framework for Trauma

However, in order to locate PTG within the more robust field of trauma studies, this construct must also be placed in context of a preexisting theoretical framework. Judith Herman's work has provided an over-arching theoretical and clinically applicable framework for trauma recovery, that can serve to anchor what the construct of PTG can offer. Specifically, Herman's framework for trauma occurs in three stages (1997). The first, is the stage of safety, the second is remembrance and mourning, and the third is reconnection. Each of these stages is necessary to the healing process, and individuals typically vacillate between the three stages at different points in their journey toward healing.

The first stage, the stage of safety, involves establishing a physical and emotional baseline for regulating oneself, so that a person is able to access their higher psychological faculties. A person who is experiencing flashbacks, or is still too physically close to the cause of trauma, is unable to fully participate in restorative psychological treatment due to the constant, and perhaps even dissociating nature of their hyperarousal. If the body is not physically safe, or if the stimuli that triggers a re-experiencing of the trauma are too imminent, the work of grief, narration, and meaning-making will be nearly impossible. For Herman, "establishing safety begins by focusing on control of the body and gradually moves outward toward control of the environment" (p. 160). This includes obtaining appropriate medical care/treatment, regaining healthy biorhythms of eating and sleep, and minimizing the intensity of intrusive symptoms through the use of therapeutic grounding, and possibly medication. Additionally, this stage can require major life changes that distance the individual from a toxic, unsafe, abusive, or re-traumatizing environment. These basic needs precede any capacity for narrative extension that may eventually promote PTG. Though it is possible that creative activity and more basic types of art therapy may be useful in reconnecting an individual with a sense of mastery, control and self-soothing, the existential, reflective, and meaning-making aspects of the healing process are not the goal at this stage (Rankin & Taucher, 2011; Herman, 1997). Rather, the goal is to establish a baseline for physiological regulation and physical protection so that deeper healing and recovery can eventually take place.

The second stage in which deeper healing begins, is the stage of remembrance/mourning (1997). This stage, for Herman, is where the narrative of the trauma takes place. In telling the "story of the trauma . . . in depth and in detail" "reconstruction (that) actually transforms the traumatic memory (begins) so that it can be integrated into the survivor's life story" (p. 175). While telling this story, the therapeutic relationship provides a resource to empower the individual by being both a "witness and ally" (p. 175). The narrative of the trauma must include the details of pre-trauma life, the imagery and physical senses encased in the trauma, and a re-experiencing of the primary emotions involved in the incident. In doing so, it is crucial to gravitate back to safety needs whenever an individual becomes too dysregulated to fully participate in the narrative work as a conscious and free agent participating in the change.

As the work of building a narrative proceeds within a context of safety, this may prompt existential questions, a deeper and more complex search for meaning-making (Park et al., 2017). As such a narrative develops, and existential question emerges, the simultaneous experience of a grief and mourning are typically inevitable (Herman, 1997). If an individual is going to build new neurological and affective pathways that can incorporate experiences of safety and meaning, towards new experiences of agency and empowerment, the blockages created by grief and loss have to be navigated, and worked through in an attuned, sensitive and mindful way (Cozolino, 2010; Herman, 1997; Van der Kolk, 2014).

The fluctuation between safety needs, integration of memory and new experience at this stage can be incredibly raw, and requires clinical sensitivity, mutual courage and thoughtful balancing. Contextually, this is the stage where any potential for PTG can begin, as this creates a broader, deconstructive space where the tension between trauma and future possibility reside. This may also be a stage in which more projective, broad and emotionally laden creative expression may be most useful. Art-therapist and neuroscientist Noah Hass-Cohen (2008; 2016) describes the importance of both "creative embodiment" and "transformative integrating" in processing traumatic and emotional pain in her Art Therapy Relational Neuroscience (ATR-N) model. "Creative embodiment" is the mindful attention of connected bodily senses during the action of creating, almost existing as a form of self-reflective biofeedback that arises during physical acts of creating. For Hass-Cohen, this creative embodiment leads to adaptive, artistic emergence of repressed, or even dissociated material, that leads to a "transformative integrating" in the brain and body; bringing a salve to traumatic memories by embedding new, self-controlled experiences of deliberate action. Creative embodiment can become a progressive, scaffolded experience after safety has been established.

When reconciled with the second stage of remembrance/mourning Herman's (1997) model, creative bodily action engages the physical senses and repressed or dissociated emotional material by layering paint, shaping and trimming sculptures, etching designs, immersing oneself in landscape photography, and experimenting with a variety of perspectives and intonation in dancing and music. Different affects, sensations, perspectives, and facets of the self are given expression through the body on a physiological, and unconscious level.

Transformative integrating is the following step according to Hass-Cohen (2008), and includes putting words to or building a narrative around one's artistic or creative process. Pairing narrative and creative action builds upon the intrapsychic and relational connections, as well as the capacity for meaning-making that is involved in trying to reengage the variety of thoughts, feelings, images and senses that can become stifled and even frozen from traumatic experiences. In essence, the centrality of Herman's second stage is perhaps the most psychologically painful, but also provides crucial opportunity for experiential application, both in terms of creative engagement, and even kindling the potential for PTG.

Herman's last stage, however, represents the goal of healthy processing and movement forward from traumatic constriction. This stage is the stage of "reconnection," and is a result of "coming to terms with the traumatic past . . . and (facing) the task of creating a future," and "reclaims (their) world" by developing a "new self," "new relationships," and finding "anew a sustaining faith" (1997, p. 196). This stage is the result of having understood the nature of their trauma, working through it, and locating ways in which to understand and self-regulate traumatic triggers in a way that conditions a sense of confidence. The traumatic survivor is now empowered to protect themselves, reach out to others for help when needed, and may even empower and empathize with others in a powerful way. While Herman notes that trauma is never "completely" (p. 211) resolved, reconnection signals that significant healing has taken place so that a survivor's life can become both more "ordinary" and more "adventurous" (p. 203), resembling Winnicott's (1971) description of play as "the natural thing" (pp. 38, 39) to do. Hypothetically, this stage would be related to the most observable outgrowth of any positive change after trauma, and would be were PTG would be most observable and reflective if it occurs for a person.

Precipitants of Growth

What Herman described in the stage of reconnection, is essentially the fruit of the arduous journey of recovery. While reconnecting with a full life is the goal in trauma treatment, the process of the journey can change people (Herman, 1997). This change, when it manifests as positive reconnection, is largely what Calhoun and Tedeschi (1998; 2013) have attempted to capture in the construct of PTG. But the experience of PTG within an individual's trajectory of healing and recovery is not a given. Rather, the range of sample populations reporting aspects of positive change after a trauma range from 30% all the way up to 90%, which details enormous variance in its occurrence (Calhoun & Tedeschi, 2006). Further, many individuals who report PTG also report aspects of inhibited living, or "depreciation" in the very areas that they have experienced growth (Baker et al., 2008). This can be seen in the individual who experiences a deterioration in their faith, in their personal relationships, and in their ability to appreciate life after a trauma. In such a case, the five domains of growth are harmed in the meaning-making process (Park et al., 2017). Baker and colleagues note that "people (appear to) keep 'scores' for both the positive and negative changes they perceive in themselves" (2008, p. 461) when confronted with making meaning of their world after a trauma. An example would be an individual who, after surviving a flood and losing their house, reports having grown to appreciate life more—in the form of gratitude for family—but also reports that their journey after this trauma has simultaneously caused a negative impact in their appreciation for life on a separate item list, perhaps in the form of disappointment with state governmental aide. This simultaneous occurrence of growth and depreciation reflects that though PTG can be of great utility, it may also be a difficult resource to harness.

One way to harness this complexity, is to better account for the predictors of variance in the reports of PTG. Thus far, such predictors of PTG are numerous, and include a range of attributes, characteristics and behaviors. A steadily established and central predisposing predictor of growth is the intensity of distress caused by a traumatic event (Bellizzi & Blank, 2006; Morris et al., 2005; Wild & Paivo, 2016; Xu & Liao, 2011). The finding that higher levels of growth are related to higher intensities of traumatic distress, aligns with Janoff-Bulman's (1992) theoretical stance, which suggests that in order to truly reorganize space for expansive growth, an assumed worldview must be shaken to its very foundation. This is not to say that the intensity of traumatic incident is inherently "beneficial," as depreciation and posttraumatic stress may be higher as well. Rather, this is to simply highlight that those individuals who report the most growth tend to have had to do the most rebuilding of their previously held worldviews. The upending of such worldviews may be a result of higher subjectively traumatic experience, which is why it is possible to report elevated symptoms of posttraumatic stress, alongside elevated reports of PTG (Calhoun & Tedeschi, 2006; Cann et al., 2011).

Such findings are not limited to acute trauma, but include long-term adaption from traumatic experience, and suggest unique moderators. A study in breast cancer survivors (Bellizi & Blank, 2006) found that higher intensity of the disease, adaptive coping, and younger age all predicted higher levels of PTG. Similarly, a study of survivors of the 2008 earthquake in Sichuan, China, found PTG to be significantly higher for females, younger age, more formal education, and higher levels of initial distress and proximity to the natural disaster (Xu & Liao, 2011). Danahauer and colleagues discovered that for individuals who had received a leukemia diagnosis, younger age, more time since diagnosis, and more intense challenges of core beliefs all predicted elevated growth (2013). Prati and Pietrantoni (2009) found positive reappraisal and religious coping to both predict PTG, with gender and age serving again as moderating factors. The combined facets of these studies may suggest a unique interplay between direct distress severity and coping ability, with moderating impacts of gender, age and education. While high distress severity and more positive forms of coping are related to the empirical and theoretical underpinnings of how growth occurs (see Janoff-Bulman, 1992); the correlation of younger age, female gender, and higher education with higher PTG may indicate cognitive and characterological trends that inform PTG as a construct. Such trends may suggest that dimensions of greater social, emotional, and cognitive flexibility provide a stronger foundation for growth.

Social, emotional and cognitive flexibility may function as structural predictors in some cases, and attitudinal postures, in others which can promote constructive meaning making. Calhoun and Tedeschi affirm that individuals who display hope, optimism, "an open, complex cognitive style," a "tendency towards action," and a baseline of a "modest (sense) of control over their lives" are more likely to experience growth (1998, pp. 224–26). It seems vital to find intentional and practical applications in order for trauma survivors to experience growth. A longitudinal study beginning in early stages of breast cancer diagnosis, demonstrated significant relationship between positive reappraisal coping and PTG, but no link between PTG and benefit finding (i.e., identifying areas of benefit from distressful experience; Sears et al., 2003). This at first may appear like a dissonant finding, since benefit finding would seem more conceptually resonant with growth. But the key factor seems to be the ability to cope in a way that gives space to creatively reframe, and actively engage perceptions of growth into the rhythm of a person's life. Intellectualizing potential benefits of emotional and physical adversity does not appear to be enough.

Again, the importance of creative and adaptive coping may be connected to why self-reports of gratitude have been found to predict greater levels of PTG (Vieselmeyer et al., 2016). An experience such as gratitude may be superior to "benefit finding" because gratitude is an activated, emotionally salient practice, that moves beyond rote rehearsal. It seems to be a posture that creatively accesses a new perspective with resonating affect. Calhoun and Tedeschi (1998) highlight such intentional, creatively generated coping, as a variable preceding growth. Drawing upon Sternberg (1985) and Strickland (1989) they conclude that more creative coping utilizes unconventional worldviews, constructive cognitive flow, and mindful attention to nuance, all the while holding a degree of flexibility and individuality. Alongside the moderating factors of female gender, younger age (Bellizi & Blank, 2006; Danahauer et al., 2013; Prati & Pietrantoni, 2009; Xu & Liao, 2011), and the direct effects of higher pre-trauma emotional health, and higher levels of traumatic distress, "creative coping" appears to all cater towards positive change with common theoretical mechanisms.

Research has indeed established some functional differences between PTG, resilience, and coping, but the instances of conceptual overlap can be difficult to tease apart (Stanton & Low, 2004; Prati & Pietroni, 2009; Vieselmeyer et al., 2016). For the sake of simplification, resilience will be defined as the ability to persevere through challenging, but non-traumatic events without breakdown (Connor, 2006; Sears et al., 2003); coping as the thoughts and behaviors that help a person deal with the immediate stress of that difficulty (Lazarus, 1999; Rodriguez-Rey et al., 2016), and growth as an emergent phenomenon which comes after a trauma of enough intensity to disrupt one's worldview (Tedeschi & Calhoun, 1998).

Vieselmeyer and colleagues (2016) identify the differences between resilience and growth, showing that while resilience protects against higher levels of posttraumatic stress, it does not elicit a main effect on PTG (2016). Similarly, Prati and Pietratoni (2009) performed a meta-analysis from a total of 103 different studies to look at the effects of optimistic attitudes, social support, and various coping strategies in relationship to PTG. Their findings suggested the large effects for PTG are found in coping—but only very specific forms of coping. Notably, religious forms of coping, and coping that construes circumstances with positive reappraisal were the most impactful, while coping via acceptance had the least impact towards PTG. In respect to such studies the case can be made that growth can benefit from a baseline of resilience and positive coping, but neither resiliency nor coping ability clearly accounts for PTG in and of itself. Perhaps the best illustration to differentiate PTG from other variables can be found in budding life visible in the five domains of PTG.

Domains of PTG

Postraumatic growth is not a one-dimensional entity but a group of characteristics—a variety of blossoming "leaves" or "petals"—that makes up a new floral emergence of growth. The essential characteristics, being the "leaves" or "petals," of posttraumatic growth have been shown to fall within five distinct, factored domains (Baker et al., 2008; Morris et al., 2005, Tedeschi & Calhoun, 1998). These domains assess for change in (1) *New Possibilities*, (2) *Relating to Others*, (3) *Personal Strength*, (4) *Spiritual Change*, and (5) *Appreciation for Life*; and are related to three broader concepts of change which involve shifts in sense of self, relationships, and philosophy of life (Calhoun & Tedeschi, 2013). Noting these domains helps give the phenomenon of PTG distinguished weight within multiple facets of a trauma survivor's life. Each domain centrifugally reflects aspects of positive change. The importance of these self-reported domains of growth are inherently value-laden and may be difficult to subjectively quantify in every instance, but these self-reports are also important markers for transformative change.

First, the domain of *New Possibilities* is related to the development of new interests, mining for the connection between a disrupted worldview, and a renegotiation of that worldview that primes new ways of engaging in the world. Peterson and colleagues (2008) found significant partial correlations between PTG and character strengths of creativity, curiosity, and new learning, which they theoretically connect to the level of openness that comes from new possibility. New possibilities prompt a vision toward emerging connectedness, that is fundamental to artistic disciplines, and can be a product of playful encounter.

Second, *Relating to Others*, involves a renovation of the self as related to others, that promotes a broader capacity for compassion, indicating an emotional form of creative empathy that stimulates new levels of mutuality. Many who have experienced PTG have shared that through confronting their tragic experiences, they were led to a more demonstrative connection with others, including a more potent compassion extended for suffering in the world. This has been qualitatively linked in the narratives of interviews to higher degrees of altruism, as well as increased authenticity, intimate sharing, a liberated sense of harmony and even higher likelihood of personal disclosure (Calhoun & Tedeschi, 2006).

Third, *Personal Strength* searches for the emergent quality of self-reflection, that requires a renewed portrayal of self as more resourceful, and resilient than previously imagined. Character strengths like bravery, honesty, and perseverance have also been found to link with post traumatic growth, and conceptually align with this domain (Peterson et al., 2008). The experience of disclosure in the congruent shape of artistic, creative and playful expression can be an act of bravery and acceptance that is profound, and invigorating for a person's sense of strength after tragedy.

Fourth, *Spiritual Change* involves a subjective improvement in a sense of metaphysical interconnectedness, embedding self-experience with deeper, more nuanced, approach to reality as a whole. This change is not unlike the shift of artistic vision, that can integrate all aspects of life into a more transcendent field of meaning. Observations by Calhoun and Tedeschi led them to conclude that for some individuals, change in existential, religious or spiritual aspects of life are the most formidable areas of growth after trauma (2006).

Fifth, *Appreciation for Life*, seeks to detail the widened quality of living that a person may approach with freshness, holism, and spontaneous wonder that is so often dormant without creative intercession. Character strengths reported by Park and colleagues (2017) that align with this domain include the experience of gratitude, appreciation of beauty, and zest for life. As these domains come together in the broader concepts of self, relationships and philosophy of life, they detail an approach for change that emphasizes emergent action and connection between self, others and the world. This connection mirrors an artists' practice, much like an internal rendering of renewed subjectivity experienced through playful reshaping of a sculpture, layered painting, a redefined story arc, or honed dance style.

The domains of growth *New Possibilities, Relating to Others, Personal Strength, Spiritual Change* and *Appreciation for Life,* can be considered hallmarks of rich living and personal expansion. The capacity to enhance these areas of life in working through traumatic turmoil provides a profound and hopeful message for those who have survived dire circumstances. Widening the breadth of such change, and clinical application, through the resource of creativity presents a glimmer of light to those who are stuck in ruminative processes. It is a clinician's duty, not only to hold out for such hope and light alongside his/her clients, but it is also a clinician's privilege to see individual creative expression yield personal growth. These domains hypothetically may be difficult to observe until Herman's (1997) final stage of reconnection, but they may be powerfully accessed in moments during the second stage of remembrance and mourning. The domains of growth may expand, especially if such remembrance and mourning can be encountered through creative agency, in a way that facilitates a constructive reprocessing or "deliberative rumination," which will be discussed later in this chapter.

PHYSIOLOGICAL CORRELATES OF TRAUMA AND CREATIVITY

The potential for art-making and creative expression to benefit trauma recovery, and perhaps even growth in the reconstructive process, has various theoretical, empirical and neuropsychological precedence. In order to accentuate the use of creativity for promoting PTG, existing research of shared physiological structures and resonance between trauma, creativity, and experiential growth will be described. This will include describing the interplay between trauma and creativity in hemispheric lateralization, as well as the roles of narrative, and art-making in trauma treatment (Van der Kolk, 2003). The neurophysiological correlation between trauma treatment and art therapy is embellished in the five core domains of change measured in the construct of PTG. These five core domains of PTG (*New Possibilities, Appreciation for Life, Personal Strength, Relating to Others* and *Spiritual Change*), could surface, manifest and encode through creative processes, within the oscillating context of Herman's stages of remembrance and mourning, and reconnection. But in order for such growth to emerge, traumatized individuals must first learn to safely navigate the overwhelming and disorienting impact of hemispheric lateralization, through gradual experiences of neural and hemispheric integration.

Hemispheric Lateralization and the Nervous System

Traumatic incidents can have a visceral impact on the brain, nervous system, and emotional regulatory capacities (Van der Kolk, 2003). In addition, the overlap and interaction between chronic and acute traumas across the lifespan can incite complex trauma, which can be insidiously difficult to treat given the developmental, interpersonal and recurring nature of such trauma (Courtois & Ford, 2009; Gallegos & Hillbrand, 2016). However, what all forms of trauma have in common is the resulting constriction and dysregulation of the self—resulting in emotional, physical and relational fallout (Van der Kolk, 2014). Consequently, the collective fallout of trauma can recreate the helplessness, paralysis and terror, upending a person's ability to reintegrate into healthy rhythms of life in a balanced, and empowering way.

Bessel van der Kolk (2003) describes that this is why "traumatized individuals need to have experiences that directly contradict the emotional helplessness and physical paralysis" involved in trauma (p. 188). Van der Kolk (2003), like Herman (1997), emphasizes that in order to promote healthy and regulated functioning, individuals must be able to experience and internalize their own capacity to find safety, regulate hyperarousal, and emotionally connect for treatment to be effective. The fractured memories and triggers of trauma can form a lateralization of the brain's right and left hemispheres, similar to an asymmetrical gap in the tectonic plates of the mind-body connection, creating friction and disturbance (Konopka, 2015).

Lateralization increases arousal within the right hemisphere, resulting in over-activation of the "amygdala, the insula, and the medial temporal lobe," and simultaneous decrease in the "activation of the left inferior frontal lone" or "Broca's area" (Van der Kolk, 2003, p. 185; see also Shapleske et al., 1999). This is significant because the Broca's area is involved in moving experiences into language. So, while hemispheric lateralization increases the emotional and corresponding physiological stress-response, it decreases the ability for a person to communicate what is happening to them, which may create a self-reinforcing pattern of flooding. Though the impact of lateralization is more complex than a simple two-way, cause-effect pattern, it is still generally crucial to treating trauma. Konopka (2015) reviews:

> Because of the inherent plasticity of the brain and its adaptation to the environment including pathology, the concept of

pure hemispheric lateralization is modified as new data emerge, however, in general, neuroscientists have discovered that the left hemisphere plays a special role in language comprehension and controls movement on the right side. Conversely, the right hemisphere specializes in perception and synthesis of nonverbal information including music, facial expression, and movement of the left side of the body. (p. 25)

The constricting and paralyzing nature of trauma, and consequent lateralization, inhibits the neurological capacity to successfully integrate thoughts, emotions and memories in tandem. Neurological integration between hemispheres is central to trauma recovery, and may also implicated in varieties of creative processes, verbal articulation of narrative, and relationships (Hass-Cohen & Findlay, 2015). So, while the trends in hemispheric differences are well-established, the road to healing may take many paths that connect language, emotion, memory bodily movement, visual and auditory perception, in order to promote hemispheric integration through new experiences of safety and reconnection (Herman, 1997).

Additionally, from a physiological standpoint, clinicians must also account for the interaction between the parasympathetic and sympathetic nervous systems in traumatic exposure, and its impact on lateralization (Koss & Trantham, 2013; Lee et al., 2014). Porges (2011) proposes that there is a strong bodily response in the sympathetic nervous system to danger, and the role of the parasympathetic nervous system, particularly involving the mutual activity of dorsal and vagal vagus nerve complexes, may illuminate adaptive stress responses. Such adaptive processes in humans can take place through positive social-emotional feedback, and attachment cueing that are unique to the human makeup in the ventral vagus nerve complex. In this way, Porges (2011) suggests that narrative, social relationships, emotional containment and constructive agency (rather than sympathetic reactions) may form a protective network of resources to promote safety, narrative processing, and reconnection simultaneously. This utilizes the natural plasticity of the brain to work towards health, and optimally will also be a highly personal, attuned and individualized process.

Konopka reminds readers that "Despite the brain's highly specialized neuronal circuits, we know that there are no absolutes for brain function; brain function is as unique as individuals" (2015, p. 33). It appears that in some respect, neuroscience demystifies a world of complexity involved in trauma response, but at the same time furthers attention towards the complexity of individual processes. This sentiment may highlight the irre-placeable nature of attuned interpersonal empathy, reflective intuition and mirroring that can buffer each stage of trauma recovery.

The highly personal nature of trauma, requires highly attuned inter-personal responsiveness from others in a trauma survivor's community and network of care (Ogden et al., 2006). Herman's (1997) stage of safety (changing one's immediate environment, learning grounding techniques, etc.) serves as a place to stabilize the body and mind so that the benefits of attuned therapy can work toward such neural plasticity by scaffolding ex-periences, and internalization of containment. For Winnicott (1965; 1971), this is the necessary holding environment which establishes the bounds of safety that allow the relational space to become therapeutic.

The need for such personally attuned support, leads to one of the most pivotal aspects of care in psychotherapy and trauma recovery—the sharing of the trauma narrative. PTG domains of *New Possibilities, Appreciation for Life, Personal Strength, Relating to Others* and *Spiritual Change* could po-tentially all be heightened during the process of promoting neural plastic-ity, and decreasing hemispheric lateralization, through personalized care, attuned affirmation, and construction of narrative. Narrative in a way is the conscious meaning-making that stems from the unconscious affect and memory Winnicott's (1971) holding environment hopes to tease out, and integrate through spontaneous activity, free association and play. For Her-man, narrative is often the critical beginning to the stage of remembrance and mourning (1997).

Narrative and PTSD

The importance of sharing one's narrative after trauma as a step to recovery is hard to overstate. The centrality of narrative is perhaps best captured in Herman's stage of remembrance and mourning, as an irreplaceable step toward healing (1997). Specific interventions like Narrative Exposure Ther-apy (NET) have even been shown to significantly decrease PTSD symp-toms, suggesting that this practice may be pivotal in the recovery process (Adenauer et al., 2011; Neuner et al., 2004). This is a promising starting point for buffering the type of neurological integration described above, which reduces the impact of hemispheric lateralization and acuity of stress responses. Drawing on Cozolino (2010), art therapist and neuroscientist Noah Hass-Cohen argues that treatment of PTSD must help an individual build emotional and conceptual coherence, with sensitivity to the "temporal, causal, thematic, and cultural dimensions" (Hass-Cohen & Findlay, 2015, p. 143) of a traumatic memory. This is precisely the role of narrative, as the use of autobiographical memory can unlock sensory memories held in the body while extending them into new conscious and self-reflective memories. So, narrative can work to mutually build coherence, while providing an expressive voice for the affective and organizational elements of grappling with pain, amending memories in a new context of containment and personal agency (Hass-Cohen & Findlay, 2015; Van der Kolk, 2014).

However, working through a trauma narrative is a complex clinical task, that requires sensitive gauging of the client's need for safety (Herman, 1997). If the process moves too quickly, it may reinforce the subjective feeling of fear, eliciting an overwhelming physiological response that may quickly backfire (Fosha, 2003; Herman, 1997; Tripp, 2016; Van der Kolk, 2014). This is why Herman's establishment of basic emotional and physiological grounding is key for moving into deeper stages of trauma work. Narrative remembrance and physiological grounding must be woven together.

Van der Kolk (2014) agrees, identifying two prominent aspects of self-awareness that aid trauma recovery. These aspects are autobiographical, and moment-to-moment self-awareness. Autobiographical awareness accesses the sense of self through time, and engages both an individual's memory and language in narrative, since "narratives change with our telling, as our perspective changes and as we incorporate new input" (p. 238). Self-awareness in moment-to-moment, however, largely attends to physical sensations (Kelley et al., 2002). Both forms of awareness, described by Van der Kolk (2014), may benefit from simultaneous and oscillating activation. Bodily awareness and the autobiographical self might both be accessed through creative activity, which allows for the temporal and immediate aspects of traumatic exposure to be integrated (Hass-Cohen & Findlay, 2015).

Hass-Cohen and Findlay (2015) break down such powerful implications, emphasizing the possibility for representational arts therapy to help reconsolidate autobiographical narrative. They state:

> Art representations contribute to accessing and making events, vivid, coherent and enduring. As the work progresses, the media properties, combined with creating and making meaning, decrease affective numbing and soothe aroused responses in the here and now. These adaptive states, which are supported by

the client labeling and narration of the art further empower clients ... [while] fostering contextualization and updating autobiographical memory. . . . [Furthermore] engaging therapeutic and pleasurable art making while confronting internal fear responses exercises novelty and reward-based processes. Meanwhile, imagining an optimistic image of the future creates a sense of parasympathetic calm and a view of a future self. (pp. 147–48)

In this way, the aspects of bodily grounding, meaning-making, pleasure, and memory function can be interlocking elements of narrative displayed through creative forms.

Art Therapy and Trauma

While art therapies are a "well-established therapy (in facilitating) nonverbal emotional expression and therapeutic communication" (Konopka, 2015, p. 26) they might also benefit and empower Herman's stage of remembrance (1997). This might occur by accessing memories while simultaneously building new experiences, leading to more intentional self-reflective processing of a traumatic event and its effects which Calhoun and Tedeschi (2015) refer to as deliberative rumination. New experience is crucial to Herman's stage of reconnection, because it allows the trauma survivor to engage fuller living, moving on from tragedy and into the possibility of transformation, and a hopeful future. As previously stated, creative arts may assist the trauma recovery process by undoing the effects of hemispheric lateralization, extending a more robust narrative post-trauma, and insulating more regulated bodily responses (Crenshaw, 2006; Koss & Trantham, 2013; Van der Kolk, 2014). The traditional roles of art therapy have a pronounced clinical history for facilitating trauma recovery, hypothesized by Koss and Trantham (2013) to stem from strengthening mindful self-composure, more adaptive coping, and unraveling the caustic effects of emotional suppression reinforced in traumatic experience. The primary pathways in which art therapy can facilitate recovery from trauma are suggested to include both "bottom-up" and "top-down" processes (Fosha, 2003; Fosha, 2009; Hass-Cohen & Findlay, 2015; Koss & Trantham, 2013). Bottom-up and top-down processes mutually entail a variety of art-making approaches for different aspects of treatment and individualized needs, and might specifically impact the domains of New Possibilities and Personal Strength measured in PTG.

Hass-Cohen and Findlay (2015) describe bottom up change as consolidation of sensory input, that helps strengthen adaptive inter and intra-lobe connections within the brain. Such capacity for adaptions of sensory experience, and corresponding neural change, has been demonstrated in individuals who lose one sense, (i.e., vision or hearing) and it heightens and expands another sense (Collignon et al., 2013). For example, an individual who loses the sense of sight can cultivate an adaptive consolidation of the senses of hearing and touch. Bottom-up change is experiential, bodily, and manifests as neural integration.

Top down change involves the memory, attention and learning involved in processes like learning an instrument, and practicing mindfulness, which allows an individual quicker and automatic access to learned activities. Top-down change requires intentional mental focus and practice, and therefore strengthens the potential for mental intentionality to effect bodily responses. A superficial, and very generalized summary of bottom-up change is bodily and emotional experience eliciting new capacities in the brain; whereas top-down change is newly practiced mental capacities that elicit regulated responses in the body. Noah Hass-Cohen's Art Therapy Relational Neuroscience (ATR-N) model was actually developed specifically to bring together bottom-up and top-down change in art therapy to foster resilience, in a neurobiologically informed model (2008).

While this model is not specifically aimed at treating trauma, it connects the neuroscience of resilience, attachment and mindfulness to address a wide range of therapeutic needs. Her approach to therapy has tremendous overlap with processes required for working through, and making meaning from trauma. Hass-Cohen & Findlay (2015) argue that such an approach not only may assist trauma recovery, but "creates a contagious social energy and supportive, sensorial group experience" in which "expressive visual approaches provide gateways to learning the complexities of neuroanatomy" (2015, pp. 1–2). Bottom-up and top-down processing are nested within a relational framework in the ATR-N model, which could make it especially applicable to PTG (2008).

Top down change occurs as they practice new forms of attention and learning that is intentional, step-wise and is built upon executive functioning, while bottom-up change may occur automatically as individuals interact directly with artistic media (Hass-Cohen & Findlay, 2015). Top-down processing could specifically renew a sense of possibility and personal strength, given the focus on self-controlled decision making and experiential learning. Bottom-up change, which is the more automatic immersive experiential approach, could harness the unconscious and emotive capacities involved in attachment and self-expression. Together, Hass-Cohen and Findlay expand the link of bottom-up and top-down processes by emphasizing a relational framework for the ATR-N approach, in which sharing the art-making process with others, accelerates the therapeutic process by building on the neurobiology of attachment.

It is suggested that bottom-up approaches may mobilize the dormant material, while top-down processes bring an explicit constructive reformation of narrative (Hass-Cohen & Findlay, 2015). Given the risks of bottom-up approaches accessing dormant, embodied traumatic material, this is not recommended until the stage of safety is firmly established with access to both a therapist at regular intervals, and a variety of self-regulation and de-escalation techniques (such as grounding, deep breathing, and a safety plan) have been established. Hass-Cohen and Findlay emphasize that once safety is established, moving from more unconscious, abstract communication, to more conscious representational communication can function as an experience of psychological scaffolding through the creative arts. Two bottom-up interventions suggested for eliciting unconscious emotions include Scribble Drawing and Decalomania. During scribble drawing a client is encouraged to make spontaneous marking with a pencil, and allow their body to speak without intention, accessing movement patterns, shading, and shape as they naturally arise. Decalomania, on the other hand, a client pours dark paint from a cup with an angled rim to dribble paint on a larger piece of paper on the floor, allowing individual to access physical spontaneity and form, moving "back and forth from conscious to unconscious" (p. 181), incorporating whole body movement. If such emotionally laden exercises also provide gratification and release of self-expression, the intervention is doubly useful. Both scribble drawing and decalomania are similar to Winnicott's squiggle technique (1971), but are also inspired surrealism (e.g., Jackson Pollock, Max Ernst) according Hass-Cohen.

Creators are invited to observe the work they have begun, noting a symbolism, imagery or affect that stands out. Clients explore unconscious expression by continuing to create it: through shaping, coloring, texture, and even interpreting their own physical responses to what they have started— similar to using a Rorschach blot, but the form is continuously made and elaborated upon. Such improvisational styles of art-making could bring out interconnected fears, hopes, dreams and feelings that rework a new field of possibility and that can become frozen after traumatic experiences. Having a self-experience of such creativity may also dis-embed old narratives, so new narratives can begin to emerge. It furthers the potential to move back and forth between inner reflection, and personal communication.

Top-down interventions empower decision making and executive functioning (Hass-Cohen & Findlay, 2015). One recommended intervention is mindful figure drawing. The use of mindful breathing, moving meditation, and connecting the practice of body scan with figure drawing can "synthesize . . . cognitive functions such as attention and insight with somatic experiences, tactile experiences, emoting, motivation, and motor control" (p. 346). Neural integration between hemispheres and decreased lateralization can mutually occur in mindful figure drawing, as it neural integration is experientially accessed in creating, while the meditative flowing aspect of the process could soften the effects of lateralization. This might even affect longer-term creative capacities by building mindful attunement in the practice of art making. The domains of *New Possibilities* and *Appreciation for Life* may be simultaneously activated as mindfulness attends to the subtleties of the present moment. Mindful attention can help a person tune in to details that they might otherwise miss, especially when caught up in intrusive thoughts and catastrophic fears that trauma can induce. This top-down oriented practice could open up the channels of possibility for new experience, which might manifest as a newfound appreciation for sensory experience, nature, the arts or other people. Whether mindfulness is cued by what is happening in one's hands, fingers or body, in noticing textural detail, color hue, or accent of shape and form, it might strike awe and wonder that works against paralytic emotions and intrusive thoughts.

MECHANISMS OF CHANGE AND CREATIVITY

Both bottom-up and top-down approaches to art-therapy offer paths that may allow PTG to arise. While the interactive, symbolic, storied and emotional nature of art therapy has already been reinforced through neuroscience and years of clinical application, the construct of PTG has very limited, theoretical and empirical introduction within the world of art therapy. It may however, have powerful implications for creative processes (Kaufman & Gregoire, 2016). Now that the physiological correlates and several interventions for trauma treatment through the arts have been highlighted, the mechanisms of change, that have been hinted at above, hypothesized to underlie PTG will be related to the creativity. Again, the theoretical nature of this hypothesis is limited, given aspects of controversy surrounding the validity of whether self-reported PTG is always experientially encoded into sustainable change, or whether it is, for some individuals, a defensive or biased perception (Jones, 2010).

However, more recent studies which have attempted to address the complexity of posttraumatic effects, by including the construct of post-traumatic depreciation (PTD) in tandem with PTG (Cann et al., 2010; Forgeard, 2013). The hope is that measuring PTG and PTD simultaneously establishes a more robust theory which compensates for many of the limitations and complexities that arise in self-measurements of posttraumatic phenomena. Though clinicians must attend to PTD, there are three clinical mechanisms that have been suggested that aid cultivation of any PTG that might arise in an individual's process of recovery.

Throughout the process of cultivating potential PTG are three key clinical mechanisms of change—expert companionship, constructive self-disclosure and meaning making, and intrusive and deliberative rumination (Calhoun & Tedeschi, 2013). Each of these mechanisms of change might be engaged, sharpened, and reshaped in a variety of creative processes (Calhoun & Tedschi, 2013; Cann et al., 2011; Park et al., 2017; Triplett et al., 2012; Winnicott, 1971).

Expert Companionship

Though the predisposing factors of growth are complex, and the nutrients are varied, the "living organism" of PTG seems to have its own process of emotional and existential "photosynthesis," through specific mechanisms of change. The first mechanism, according to Calhoun and Tedeschi (2013), is the role of expert companionship. Expert companionship provides and models safety within the therapeutic relationship, while nurturing the potential for growth. An expert companion attends to the client throughout the process of recovery, and in many ways is helping "till" and "water" the soil of pre and post-trauma life through physiological grounding, empathic reflection and exploration of thematic material. In many ways, expert companionship as described by Calhoun and Tedeschi (2013), is simply a validating and empowering therapist, who offers a safe context to bear witness as emphasized by Herman (1997). However, an expert companion is not only providing a context to bear witness to tragedy, but they are also alert to bearing witness to possible growth in the reorganization process when working through a trauma.

Expert companionship models the supportive and containing role of a holding environment, helping an individual to get in touch with the fullness of their experience. This promotes the relational grounding for the spontaneous creative drive to manifest (Winnicott, 1954; Winnicott, 1971). An expert companion will help consolidate experiences of agency, energy, and sprouting life that can grow even when surrounded by destructive debris of trauma, through attendance and reflection toward a client's process of recovery. For example, as a therapist builds rapport into a collaborative empathic witnessing of the trauma, a survivor of physical assault is no longer alone, forced to manage disruptive and intrusive symptoms of the memory. The therapist may hold both the simultaneous pain of helplessness in being attacked, along with the longing for a fantasy of violent reactivity. As a companion through the full range of emotions, the formation of a holding environment may enable the client to tolerate powerful affects and confused cognitive recall, with a co-laborer and partner who has expertise in the recovery process.

Expert companionship may also be expanded through direct use and co-cultivation of creative and playful energy as it displays in small ways. This must be done while sensitively guarding the fragility of a trauma survivors subjective experience through grounding techniques, and cooperatively journeying through the many aspects of a trauma narrative (Calhoun & Tedeschi, 2013). This grounding and narrative process may integrate a variety of creative arts interventions—whether this is through bottom-up interventions like using expressive paint-dribbling of decalomania to give words to guttural experiences that are difficult to articulate; or top-down experiences such as a timeline drawing which incorporates representative details of pre and post trauma states (Hass-Cohen & Findlay, 2015). But more importantly from a growth perspective, the spontaneity accessed through the witnessing of personal creativity provided by a therapist might reconsolidate aspects of the true self in moments of renewal and discovery in play, along with the dormant moments of mourning, rage, and that can stifle the ability to play. The therapist's ability to contain, bear witness, and guide with expertise through a co-regulated navigation of the traumatic event mobilizes recovery and sets a stage for possible growth (Calhoun & Tedeschi, 2015). By providing expert companionship, the ranges of experience that are recalled or symbolized in creative process or products, may be consciously integrated into a reclamation of safety, agency, and interpersonal connection in wake of trauma.

Constructive Self-Disclosure and Meaning-Making

This leads to the second crucial mechanism of change for promoting PTG, which is the role of constructive self-disclosure. Constructive self-disclosure interacts with a reformed meaning making process through the power of personal sharing (Calhoun & Tedeschi, 2013; Park et al., 2017). These mechanisms are operationalized aspects of the narrative process, that may foster internalization of new, adaptive and meaningful self-understandings while also allowing for a controlled externalization of traumatic material.

Calhoun and Tedeschi (2013) explained that in order to be restorative this narrative must be multi-dimensional and thorough, which requires a person to work through all facets of the experience over time, until a full narrative is developed. Creativity could function as a catalyst for such a full narrative, just as described above by Hass-Cohen and Findlay (2015). Adams (2015) explained that PTG appears to occur through a "causative narrative framework" in which a trauma initiates a failure of current schema. This schema failure then prompts revision of the existing schema, and leads to an updated one, which elicits new behaviors and highlights an emergent variety of schematic and behavioral "pathways to tangible and intangible growth" (p. 111). Danhauer and colleagues (2013) observed a similar pattern in their study of patients receiving intensive treatment for leukemia. What was discovered here, was the higher degree to which the event challenged "core beliefs" (p. 21; i.e., schemas, subjective worldview, implicit understandings), the more likely PTG was to be reported.

This is hypothesized to be a result of adjusting assumptions about the nature and fragility of life, and updating them in a broader, more holistic view. From this angle, creativity may function as a priming agent for the causative narrative framework, eliciting new updates in schematic understandings of self and the world. The introduction of something as palpably embodied, visceral, and constructively pleasurable as creative activities and the arts could not only open up the bottom-up and top-down approaches self-disclosure, but they might also stimulate new systems of meaning-making (Hass-Cohen & Findlay, 2015; Kaufman & Gregoire, 2016). Meaning-making is crucial to understanding the impact, treatment, healing and longer-term after-effects of trauma, and has gained significant traction in clinical psychology in the last seventy years with the work of Viktor Frankl (1962/2006) in *Man's Search for Meaning.*

However, meaning-making is not only an engagement with vast existential questions, but also interacts with a person's interpretation of everyday life. Steger and Park (2012) proposed a meaning-making model that focuses on how people delineate significance from specific events in the lifespan, in respect to both situational (i.e., everyday experience) and global (i.e., worldview) understandings of their lives. The authors hypothesized the creative element of meaning making, can either cause further stress or facilitate recovery based upon the personal interpretation. This means that clinical sensitivity to an interpretation of an event (i.e., seeing oneself as falsely responsible for tragedy, versus, seeing oneself as a victim who has survived an atrocity), may be key to promoting PTG, rather than posttraumatic depreciation (PTD). Therapeutic assistance can be critical to discovering negatively-laden, false and potentially toxic interpretations in the recovery process, which may become destructive rather than facilitating some reclamation of self-compassion and creative agency.

In respect to PTG, Park and colleagues (2017) note that there is almost always reciprocal action in meaning-making, between spirituality, worldviews and traumatic events, which mirrors the discussion on PTG and PTD. Creative agency, in the context of genuine compassion and safety, may be more likely to load dimensionality of a trauma narrative and related self-concepts with experiences of agency, self-soothing, and rich, embodied communication. The possibility of creativity to positively impact meaning-making is similar to Hass-Cohen and Findlay's neuroscience-base model for representational art therapy. In essence, the use of representational arts therapy in trauma treatment described by Hass-Cohen and Findlay (2015), link an updated, multidimensional narrative with new creative experiences. Practices which cultivate agency have the potential to impact meaning-making, and even, possibly interact with forms of rumination after a trauma.

Intrusive and Deliberative Rumination

Even though forging paths to constructive self-disclosure and meaning-making through creative experiences might enable alternative pathways to growth; there is the inevitable risk of the traumatic material inciting dysregulated affects, thought processes and physiological responses that may cause an increase in PTSD symptomology, or even posttraumatic depreciation (PTD; Baker et al., 2008; Tedeschi & Calhoun, 1996; Tedeschi & Kilmer, 2005). This problem presents what is perhaps the most difficult and most vital aspect of facilitating PTG—the transformation of intrusive rumination into deliberative rumination. Intrusive rumination is marked by the unwanted reliving or processing of the trauma, it exacerbates stress levels and is absent of the subjective sense of agency and intentional meaning making (Calhoun & Tedeschi, 2013; Cann et al., 2011; Triplett et al., 2012). It might be likened to the residual, or entrenched social, emotional, and cognitive "shrapnel" that becomes embedded under an individual's defenses during the explosive pain and fear of trauma. This shrapnel, embedded under the defenses (i.e., an individual's threshold for coping and self-reflective processing) continues to produce painful re-experiencing and bodily memory of psychological terror. The fear memories are triggered and lead to patterns of thinking and feeling that are re-rehearsed. Often the effects of intrusive thinking related to the material associated with a trauma surface during the daily rhythms of life, interrupting a trauma survivor's capacity to live with a sense of freedom, and instead forms a sense of haunting of the incident (Herman, 1997).

Calhoun and Tedeschi (2013) note that while posttraumatic rumination is marked by intrusive thought processes organized around the trauma, deliberative rumination is a more intentional form of understanding a trauma that is similar to the process of remembrance and mourning emphasized by Herman (1997; Cann et al., 2011). Deliberative rumination, is a more intentional process in which one can express pain and confusion, helping support regulation of emotions through "constructive self-disclosure" (p. 86), and a more coherent narrative of their trauma. Ironically this difficult deliberative process can become the richest place for the promoting the possibility of PTG (Cann et al., 2011).

The power of deliberative rumination to encourage PTG is that it takes away the edge of helplessness tied to intrusive rumination, and begins to foster problem-solving, self-understanding and a re-knitting of the client's "assumptive world" (Triplett et al., 2012, p. 407). Calhoun and Tedeschi (2013) explain that "narrative must include all aspects of a client's experience, because growth does not come from denial, but from confronting the existential questions raised, and from sharing these experiences with appropriate others" (p. 103). Working traumatic experience into a larger story is pivotal in establishing subjective meaning to pain. Without this, trauma may prove to be insidious and too scary to confront, thus increasing avoidance and leaving intrusive rumination with the power to disrupt daily living. Facilitating deliberative rumination through creative means may help integrate trauma into a larger story, in a personal and embodied way.

Adjunctive, creative application, of posttraumatic experience may be a vital route for clients seeking growth in the midst of painful memories and experiences. This is because creativity can harness embodied practices, along with emotional expression, and personal narrative in a way that can integrate thoughts, feelings and self-understanding into a holistic process that addresses the intrusive and bodily effects of trauma (Koss & Trantham, 2013). Deliberative rumination—whether communicated through music, fine arts, or drama—could eventually give birth to the integration of deep, conflicting feelings that help shape a new worldview. Such a process not only makes underlying emotions more tolerable, but allows the externalization of implicit assumptions into explicit forms. The process of deliberative rumination can occur through creativity, and the process of creating may eventually yield a narrative to be articulated in therapy, with others, or with a community.

For example, the gradual development of a musical composition between therapy sessions, may over time find additional instruments, layers of dissonance and harmony, as they are suffused with the entrenched affects of an event. Such development of a musical composition may take place during quiet times when an individual is feeling deep affects that are difficult to articulate in words. This may start with recording a single guitar or piano chordal progression, or basic rhythm that captures the affects that have become stagnant. Over time (days, weeks, or months) the individual may add layers and changes to the song writing process. Perhaps as they share their creative process in a context of individual psychotherapy or expert companionship, the affects, words, sounds which they are trying to manifest shift, become sharper more specific. The tension between dissonance and harmony, the elevation in tempo, or rhythm changes in guitar work, vocals, or piano could all represent various feelings that might emerge further along in treatment; anger at injustice and hope towards the future, bitterness towards those who have violated others, longing for healing of oneself, and compassion for victims all might be articulated through sound. In the process, the traumatic affects become deliberative, and so aid what Winnicott (1971) calls the process of "decathection." Though music may require a higher level of previous expertise for such a composition, this basic direction of the work is to elaborate on surviving the incident from a new place of remembrance and empowerment, that scaffolds new concepts of self in relationship to the world—perhaps a stronger, more spiritually attuned, or compassionate sense of self.

A scaffolding of deliberative rumination may begin with memories and feelings, that works their way from the depths to the surface of cognitive expression. Engaging such contradictory feelings of guilt, panic, horror, defiant survival, shame and regret that can be attached to trauma, over time, can build a stronger capacity to regulate emotions while confronting those very triggers that threaten safety (Calhoun & Tedeschi, 2013; Herman, 1997). While having a therapist or "expert companion" is crucial in the beginning and intermediary stages of recovery, eventually the transition from the therapeutic holding emotional regulation in the outside world can be incredibly empowering in Herman's stage of reconnection.

This level of expanded emotional regulation fosters a way to disclose the trauma, decreasing the need for avoidance, and increasing the possibility for new facets of relationships to unfold. Tedeschi and Calhoun (2015) draw upon the meta-analytic study of Fratarolli (2006), who investigated over 140 self-disclosure studies, which strongly suggest that even written forms of disclosure can bring about physical and psychological benefits. It could be argued that artistic endeavors are immersive, abstract forms of self-disclosure and may correspond to similar benefits, but with a more comprehensive base of application (Hass-Cohen & Findlay, 2015; Kaufman & Gregoire, 2015). It also seems, that increasing self-disclosure in any intentional form, may simply be suited to best practice. The fruit of deliberative reflection, self-disclosure and narrative transformation can be connected to creative practices, especially in the domains in which growth happens. Self-disclosure might begin in metaphor through poetry for a person, as the bottom-up process accesses emotional states and can perhaps more seamlessly convey contradictory feelings, while sharing the meaning of a poem can become a more top-down process that extends the meanings in an organized fashion.

Creative practices, and instances of play that emerge in such practices, may also provide an outlet to strengthen deliberative rumination over intrusive forms, in an ongoing, multi-sensory setting. They may also serve as a form of self-disclosure. Studies do already support the mediating power of emotional expressiveness and expressive writing for PTG (Linley et al., 2011; Stockton et al., 2014). This resonates with the well documented research that expressive writing can buffer psychological and physical well-being (Pennebaker & Chung, 2012; Pennebaker, 1997; Pennebaker & Beall, 1986). Forgeard (2013) even found connections between PTG, and increased self-reports of creativity. Yet, studies supporting the use of creative expression, in facilitating PTG, have been nearly absent to date, even though the intersection of play and creativity can be so important for psychological development (Russ, 2004). What of dance, music, theatre, painting and freestyle spoken word? The cultural and personal options for emotional expression and bodily communication are dense with possibilities for healing, as modes of deliberative remembering. Adjunctive creative expression may function as a catalyst for deliberative rumination to slowly develop in between therapy sessions. In a way, the experience of creative play is existential bedrock for living. It is a natural resource for making sense of chaos, and communicating that which transcends self-directed communication. Inherently, the creative process, and experience of play is embodied and links the wellspring of youth to the narrative of old age. This is why there is much potency in the psychoanalytic frame of Winnicott (1953; 1965; 1971) to link creative expression to PTG: the often unconscious, embodied, spontaneous-yet-intentional space provided allows the multidimensional nature of human communication to meet the multidimensional nature of growth.

5

The Desert Rose

A Symbol for Creativity, Theology, and Posttraumatic Growth (PTG)

THIS WORK HAS ATTEMPTED to link together three phenomena: creativity, theological integration, and growth experiences amidst trauma. The central thesis of this work is that creative expression may serve as an ongoing, adjunctive therapeutic support for facilitating PTG in respect to the wider trauma recovery process. The function of creative expression in mobilizing PTG contains significant integrative theological themes and possibilities from a perspective of Christian faith, which might guide clinicians, Christian individuals, and the church as a whole. In respect to the rich, complex and wide-ranging scope of connections that can be made concerning these topics, the use of symbolism unifies the overall message with a sense of acute imagery. Using a symbol to structure the central, concluding themes of this work is congruent with Winnicott's (1971) emphasis on the power of primitive, nonverbal communication through symbolic gestures—especially concerning layered and emotionally-charged topics like trauma, development, and growth. Fortunately, the vastness, intricacy, and illuminating beauty of nature yields an opportunity for playful engagement, tangible illumination, and contemplative reflection. Playful reflection upon symbols in nature might be especially helpful when dealing with the mysteries, limitations, apparent contradictions, and surprising messages of life that exude from creativity, theology, and PTG (see Berry, 2009). This final chapter will use playful symbolism to communicate the overarching psychological and ecclesiological implications of the relationship between creativity, theology, and PTG. The symbolic "gesture" of creative symbolism will include examining the life of the *adenium obesum,* or desert rose, and the themes that carry over from the unique existence of this flora.

The desert rose will serve as the living symbol which holds together the multifaceted and emergent juxtapositions involved in the themes of creativity, theological integration, and growth after trauma. The use of this symbol is meant to be an extension of play, and could actual help co-create a future holding environment for all the theoretical systems which are interacting, and the stories of trauma, struggle, hope and growth in the people they have worked with, known or experienced personally.

The desert rose is a symbol in which the whole body of the church, clinicians and co-laborers in Christ help to nurture creativity, recovery and growth, through relationship with God, and attunement with the Holy Spirit (see 1 Cor 3:9). The desert rose—especially particular subspecies of *adenium obesum* that are native to desert ecosystems—spring up in areas with arduous and arid soil, intense heat and sunlight, and extended dry seasons (Dimmitt et al., 2009). The harsh environment of the desert is traumatic in the sense that punishing heat, impoverished soil, and lack of water, disrupt the normative possibility for most plants to survive. However, a number of desert plants have adapted root systems, and networks of nutrient storage and distribution, that not only allow them to survive, but to produce a particular beauty unique that decorate desert landscapes. Most species of desert rose develop extensive root systems underground and a correspondingly thick "caudex," or trunk, in order to survive. Out of this root system and thick caudex, stems grow and flowers blossom. Though this is technically an example of traumatic adaption, the eventual presence of the blossoming flowers is intended here to (playfully) symbolize the beauty that can emerge from traumatic chaos, as a transformative process.

For the desert rose, the trunk or caudex, which connects to the root system, has adapted and transformed over time around extreme conditions (i.e., a traumatic environmental disruption) that should stunt photosynthesis (a life-giving process); but species of desert roses have developed an expansive root system and broad caudex, to yield unique and creative life. It is not just a process of inherent resilience—though the plants have become resilient—but it is the actual transformational growth over time, that has produced sustainable life and piercing beauty despite life-threatening conditions. The desert species of adenium "preach" their survival and growth with bright, stunning, five-petaled flowers of creative majesty (see Figures 1–4 for photos of the *adenium obesum*).

Symbolically, there are three layers, and one encompassing reality, that are put on display in this picture. First, the desert rose's root system represents a sacred holding space, which is the foundation for healing and growth. Second, the caudex, or trunk, represents the body of change—which takes place through the "nutritional" mobilization of the combined use of engaged affect, honesty and creative experiences. Third, the five-petaled flower represents the manifestations of growth that are emergently formed from the process, and can also represent new displays of creativity in a person's life and the life of the community. Fourth and finally, is the one encompassing reality of the need for oxygen. Oxygen is the very breath of life (*ruach* regarding God's Spirit, *nepesh* regarding creatures that have breath) and is representative of the need for the Spirit of God to sustain life (Brueggemann, 1982; Sarna, 1989). Theologically, oxygen represents the ongoing work of the Holy Spirit, externally, and internally which is the simultaneously specific, surrounding, and incarnate power who prepares and cherishes any growth which occurs in the world. The life of the desert rose evidences resurrection power in the everyday, and the presence of beauty in an environment in which most other flowers could not survive in their initial state (for more on the Gospel in creation, Christian spirituality in nature, and the presence of the Holy Spirit in general revelation, see Berry, 2009; Johnston, 2014; Moltmann, 1992; Rohr, 2003).

Granted, every symbol has limitations, and in this case one limitation is the difference between a punishing landscape, and world-shattering events of trauma for an individual. For many people the experience of trauma is not just living in harsh, constrictive conditions and having to adapt in a transformative way, but it is an actual destruction of the landscape of life which begs for resurrection. The destruction of trauma forces one to navigate the inherent process of loss, confusion, and anger which occurs, before any possibility of growth really emerges. Yet the symbol of the desert rose, even given its imperfect symbolism and more realistic parallel to experiences of adaption to a traumatic environment, still reflects a tapestry of hope toward the possibility of transformational growth. Rather than functioning as a static symbol, the desert rose should be thought of as a living symbol—a symbol which is in process—and has undulating movement between the different layers of the organism, and layers of interaction with the outside environment. The roots, caudex, flowers and oxygenation/

respiration process each have reciprocal interactions in the life of the whole organism—which more accurately depicts the scope of trauma recovery described by Judith Herman (1997). The reciprocal interactions exist as undulating stages of safety, remembrance and reconnection in trauma recovery; and the layers of rooting, nutritional harboring, blossoming, and respiration, move back and forth, up and down, in the context of broader seasons, within the growth process and the fruit of creative emergence.

Root System as Sacred Holding Space

Connected physical space is a prerequisite for growth: and in Winnicott's terms—a holding environment is what allows for development—through emotional attunement, containment, safety, and nurturance. In gardening terms, a holding environment is equivalent to the fertile space of planting, which allows roots to branch out and dig into the soil. John Bowlby (1907–90) emphasized an interdependent psychological concept—attachment—of which he fathered the first focused observational and empirical research, which impacted the trajectory of developmental psychology and psychotherapy (Johnson, 2004; Karen, 1998; Mitchell & Black, 1995). Winnicott and Bowlby shared much in their passion for understanding infant and child development, and though their language and directions of specialty differed, many of their concepts and emphases overarch, especially concerning the importance holding and attachment in developmental formation (Kahr, 2004).

Winnicott and Bowlby share a developmental psychoanalytic perspective which elevates the bond of love above all things in preparing individuals for creative living. What both Winnicott and Bowlby communicate particularly—is the preparative vitality of steadfast love, which occurs through psychological and physical space of holding. The holding environment for Winnicott (1965; 1971), and corresponding secure attachment (Bowlby, 1968), are foundational elements of healthy maturation in the early bond between infant and caregiver which can profoundly impact the course of a lifespan (Schore, 2003). Safety in its full sense is the anchor for healthy development during the vulnerability of infancy and childhood; and this anchored holding, prepares individuals with the ability to internalize experiences of trust in themselves, and others. For Winnicott and Bowlby, love, in its reverent complexity and simplicity, grounds the rootedness of a human being's ability to live fully. This vulnerable need for safety during the grounding phase is sacred, because it reflects the holiness of God's creation—it reveals God's creative power and intent in creating humans with such dependence on relationships of love (Watson, 2003; Ulanov, 2005). Love is the condition which allows healthy roots to anchor, and branch out to endure the external realities of the natural world. Love is also the preparing element for the occurrence of life-giving play and creative action, which add beauty and meaning to the world.

The affection, attention and fidelity provided by the caretaker for the infant is neurologically symbolic of a forming root system, with all of its synaptic and biological comparisons within the human organism. For most plants, a healthy root system is not only an entry point for water and nutrients from soil, but it also is a foundation that prevents it uprooting. The holding environment for Winnicott, elicits potential space, and fosters the internalized capacity to use transitional phenomena—and undergirds what Bowlby (1968) would call a sense of a secure internal working model. Winnicott (1965; 1971) describes human attachment as taking root in the context of relational space that is mutually embodied, intrapsychic, and systemic; and like a desert plant—the strength of the roots will not only help the organism to survive the chaos and lack of predictability in the wilderness—but also to flourish later on. However, in a fractured, sinful world, vulnerability, and the primitive need for safety and holding is threatened by a variety of acute and chronic experiences of traumatic disruption.

Psychotherapy, multidisciplinary treatment, and community programs for the aftereffects of trauma must involve physiological, cognitive, emotional and existential holding space. This sacred holding space begins with developing a sense of physical and emotional safety as Herman (1997) explicitly describes in *Trauma and Recovery*. Safety empowers relational, systemic and self-regulatory formation. The issues of safety and security, however, are interdependent on a variety of factors that will be individualized for each person and their context. The sacredness of the safe or holding space, for a person who has been traumatized is palpable. This space is sacred in the sense that it is dealing with human beings who are made in God's image, in various states of acute vulnerability and need.

This vulnerable location for those made in God's very image, in many ways is a return to an acute dependency likened to the primitive location of the womb, or in the case of desert rose, the formative process of rooting, which may remain latent and indiscernible for a period of time. Every reaching root, or possible resource for emotional regulation, physical safety, empathic understanding and spiritual empowerment must be nourished to strengthen the breadth of the holding space in the context of trauma, which is often a displacement, or desert experience of the "soul" (in ancient Hebrew, soul is *nepesh*, which connotes "The whole of a person, god or creature including the body, mind, emotion, character and inner parts" (Benner, 2019; also see Sarna, 1989). However, sometimes, paradoxically, it is harsh temperatures, environment, and traumata that force roots to grow deeper, or else the entire plant will wither (Dimmit, 1997). The neurophysiological "roots" must be enabled through space that is containing, attuned and empathic enough to process truthful feelings; whether the medium is a psychotherapy office, a church gathering, a collective expressive art therapy group, a friendship or marriage, a journal, a canvas, a recording studio, or a combination of all these sorts of holding spaces, that contain sacred moments and birth understanding, hope, and power. Without a truly safe holding space for this fractured experience, the formation of neurophysiological roots of safety is stunted. However, with the presence of a transitional, holding space, a sacred process can begin to unfold into new experiences.

Concretely speaking, many churches have a small room or space dedicated as a prayer or intercessory room; which allows a focused container for prayer, meditation and worship. Bethel Church in Redding, California, has even developed a visual art-making program that is intended to be Spirit-led, functioning as a prophetic extension of ministry (2019). Combining such ideas of creative expression, intercessory prayer, and creative space might yield a specific sacred holding space, that also makes place for the apophatic expressions of spirituality: such as deconstruction, lament, and liminality; along with the experiences of prayer and potential spaces for cataphatic spirituality expressed in the affirmations and declarations of worship music, creeds, liturgy, and iconography.

The context in which sacred holding space occurs and symbolically in which roots reach down for water, is naturally communal. The environment—the soil for the desert rose, and the community for trauma survivors—becomes a critical factor to the grounding process and the ability of an individual to find both stability and nurturance. If the community functions as soil, the relational context keeps the plant from being uprooted by the chaos of weather, and also helps filter water (nurturance) to the roots (the embodied self, reaching for containment and holding). Especially when the individual is traumatized, the ability of the community can forge an avenue for relief and empowerment, rather than becoming another fracturing impediment, is critical to recovery and growth. This is the collective element of holding, and a healthily attuned, empathic, spiritually grounded community that resonates with love, hope, and the endurance of faith as the fruit of the Holy Spirit (see Gal 5:22), which provides sacred holding space.

A sacred holding space for people who have endured trauma must be generous enough to hold both ends of human experience—both the acute suffering, liminality and eventual joy—likened to the sharing in each phase of Holy Week. The meaning and function of Tenebrae (coming from the Latin for "darkness"; United Methodist Church, 2019) services, especially give space for reflection in silence, and darkness that accompany Herman's (1997) stage of trauma recovery in Mourning/Remembrance (Jones, 2010). The experiences of Maundy Thursday, Good Friday, Holy Saturday, and the hopeful light and resurrection on Easter Sunday remind, hold and contain the sacredness of liminality which births hope from a place of true freedom (Rohr, 2011). But those who have endured individual, acute, chronic, or collective trauma are given hope in knowing that Christ's suffering goes before them—and that our own human process in suffering will also, eventually, share in Christ's glory (see 1 Pet 4:13).

Caudex: Affective Engagement, Honesty, and Creativity

The adenium's root system exists below ground and is largely unseen, like most plants (Dimmit, 1997). Metaphorically this could reflect the neural connections and developmental experiences that exist below conscious awareness, in an automatic, and often primitively motivational field (Schore, 2001; Schore, 2011). But what is unique about desert species of the *adenium obesum* is not just the expansive network of roots that have stretched out under duress and aridity, but the formation of a swollen caudex, or trunk, which serves to store nutrients (see Figure 3). The large, emboldened caudex is an adaptive form of growth (or emergent transformation occurring over time) that helps the desert rose to harbor every bit of nutrition possible in a harsh climate (Dimmit, 1997).

The caudex's expansion for storage of nutrients mirrors a person's potentiality of holding onto every piece of hope, meaning, honesty, and connection that exists in the creative process when navigating trauma; and savoring those creative, emerging nutrients in the core of oneself, utilizing them to first survive, and later opening the possibility of growth. In respect to human experiences of growth after a trauma, the adenium's caudex symbolizes a storage unit for the particular nutrients of affective engagement, honesty (or truth-telling), and creative experiences. This process also vividly represents the neurophysiological process of expanding neural networks through repeated experience of simultaneously engaging affect, honesty and creativity to buffer new experiences of self, others and the world (as described by Hass-Cohen & Findlay, 2015). Affect—or genuine emotional response—must not be dissociated if healing is to occur; and society, and unfortunately both social norms and religious structures often encourage people to suppress and dissociate pain. In part, this is normative and understandable, but it also signifies systemic weakness in tolerating intense affect—which can actually be immensely powerful when a community engages traumata in a meaningfully, collective way, rather than avoiding it (especially in relative isolation, as is common in Western cultures; Saul, 2013).

Emotional suppression may inhibit genuine growth and exacerbates stress, indicating the truth of the story must be told to undo the caustic unconscious repetition of repressed trauma (Larsen & Berenbaum, 2015; Moore et al., 2008; Van der Kolk, 2014). Simultaneously, a person's true self, the self that Winnicott (1971) describes as essentially capable of play, must be able to process, discharge, and metabolize emotional experiences and traumatic stories in some personally meaningful expression. For the sake of this current work, creative expression which conveys emotional and existential meaning might be foundational for holistic change through innumerable creative forms, when they are integrated with the truth of one's experience.

Within a root system anchored in the soil of community, sacred holding can exist—as the caudex or trunk stores the emotionally salient, truthful expressions of creative communication to each unique person. These are the nutrients of Winnicott's true self in action, in recovery, and in process; it is the self that trauma inhibits, but comes alive in play. The caudex of the desert rose, in Winnicottian terms, stores the developmental experiences of play and consequent creative expressions, which helps an individual process conflicting and complex emotional, embodied experiences of dependency, fear, desire, and aggression, while returning to the genuineness and vitality of their own personhood (Ulanov, 2005; Winnicott, 1965; Winnicott, 1971). Winnicott viewed play as a process that brings the most truthful expressions, personal meaning, and creativity to the surface (1971).

However, for adults, sometimes remembering how to play, especially in the wake of trauma requires intentional self-location in a holding environment to give birth to play and concomitant creative resonance with the true self. The experiential process of constructing poetry, recording music, painting a landscape, sculpting an abstraction, composing music, collage-making, photography, or even the literal building a home, structure, garden or personal project are opportunities for transitional phenomena to take place—so long as the emotionality and genuine form of expression (play) can become infused in the process, however momentarily, subtle or overt. The experiential process is not just a solitary artistic experience, but must necessarily include at least one other attuned individual, whether that be a seasoned clinician, or in due time, a wider community. Community art-making interventions for trauma, may actually be especially powerful. Kapitan, Litell, and Torres (2011) have demonstrated that intentionally culturally-sensitive models of communal art therapies can even act as sustainable methods to empowerment and social change within traumatized and socially marginalized groups.

In church contexts, unfortunately, people harboring the emotional and physical after-effects of trauma may find themselves feeling further marginalized or alienated, depending upon implicit psychological tendencies of the religious tradition, specific community and cultural context. The hope is that the church context might actually serve as a trustworthy base for sacred holding—in which relearning how to play, and create in the midst of individual and/or collective trauma is approached with a openness and compassionate resolve, so that authentically deconstructive, and reconstructive forms of expression can take place. Just as Hass-Cohen and Findlay (2015) suggest for art therapy groups in general, the full-range of emotions need to be given a matching range of interventional space, whether that is a canvas, a journal, or the wall of building. One of the creative barriers in religious communities may be the level of public discomfort—both institutionally, and embedded within cultural variations—with negative emotional material associated with the injustices of trauma: namely emotions like rage, aggression, confusion, anger, sadness, pain and ambivalence. Transitional space for a church community must be able to provide a holding space for such an authentic range of emotional material, if it is to effect and participate in creative transformation.

Matott and Miller (2016) have exemplified papermaking art interventions for communities which have endured trauma. Drawing upon the work of Matott and Miller, art therapist Stephanie Hectorne (2017) has even extended this creative papermaking intervention for communities to establish healing dynamics within personal relationships and community dynamics, which connotes the possibility of growth. In this intervention, fabric, or paper is broken down through cutting, tearing, and blending to create fibrous pulp. The residual breakdown of elements into fibrous pulp is then shaped on a mould, deckled, couched, and designed expressively, as it dries into a new form. Entailed in the process is deconstruction, liminality, and reconstruction; and all the accompanying emotions, personal experience, and existential meaning that might be psychically and physically charged into the intervention.

A church body that hosts a space for this type of process becomes a holding environment, becoming a space which can bear witness to trauma narratives as Herman (1997) emphasizes. With this in place, the creative method—canvas, song, paper, or dance—itself becomes a microcosm of the sacred holding environment, as the broader space becomes personal and intimate. The process of breakdown infuses the aggressive and dependent drives into a deconstructive process, and in Winnicottian language, becomes an avenue of creative emergence in play, which is the declarative form of hope, renewal, and empowerment of the true self. In the current symbol of the desert rose, the intervention expands the nutritive storage of the trunk system, or caudex. Spiritually, it contains both cataphatic and apophatic expressions of intimacy with God in the process of enduring injustice, working through pain, and allowing hope to emerge in whatever light might be birthed in darkness.

Such a community-based transitional experience could take place in a dedicated space or room within a church community that is dedicated to allowing the full spectrum of creative expression, prayer, meditation, lament; held together with both affirmative and deconstructive processes. If a select "transitional" room that hosts a piano or guitar, a wall, canvas, clay and workspace might be a place where a mix of studio art and child-like emotional processing can entertain group therapy, or workshops that are directed both at grief, loss, recovery, learning, renewal, and hopeful creation in staggered, interwoven experiences throughout the day. Such a room dedicated to the permissive expression of the full experiential knowledge of each day of Holy Week that exists within each person's story, through a communally held, creative medium that best suits the spontaneous, unique personal gesture of each person, as Winnicott (1965; 1971) would emphasize. Intentional, transitional space in community, functions like a desert roses' caudex—holding onto and savoring the life-giving material that emerges in the desert.

As previously mentioned, a large percentage of this type of community-based transitional experience would occur during Herman's (1997) stage of remembrance and mourning; as the process of remembrance and mourning helps to dislodge, navigate, and work through the traumatic aftermath. But when this process is paired with experiences of creative agency and play, the nutrients of hope, meaning, truth, and expressive empowerment are stored as nutrients in the embodied "caudex" of possibility, change and transformative growth. As the nutrients of affective engagement, honesty and creative agency become stored experiences, the body of the desert rose swells in preparation for later flowering in vital reconnection, and in transformation.

Flowering: Manifestations of Growth and Creative Life

The desert rose blooms five-petaled flowers—which consist of many combinative varieties and vivid colors: pink, white, magenta, orange, black, purple, yellow and orange. These varieties are noted for their piercing beauty, and contrasting marks and hues, especially in the backdrop of the barren, brown desert landscape. The five-petaled flower is a fitting symbol of growth, especially concerning the numeric parallel with the five domains of PTG, which are *New Possibilities*, *Relating to Others*, *Personal Strength*, *Spiritual Change*, and *Appreciation for Life* (Calhoun & Tedeschi, 1998). Here, there is symbolic resonance of one petal for each domain of growth, one piece of beauty that has bloomed for each area of life, that could represent transformative phenomena of creative growth that can take place during the recovery process; in spite of the persecution, violence, and dissociative aftermath which threatens to steal the very life, joy and wholeness of a traumatized individual.

These flowers cannot bloom, without connection to the root system (holding space), and a reserve of nutrients—generated through affectively engaged, truthful, creative expression. Growth will be difficult to see without the time, and foundation of secure and loving holding that can become a sacred space for refuge, and for experiential scaffolding engaged, honest creative forms of transitional phenomena that occurs during moments of creativity and play. But when these flowers do bloom, new possibilities might begin to detail a person's worldview in the recovery process; new personal strength can be discovered in the midst of threats to one's very life; the essential value of relationships may begin to take more meaning, and become more connecting within reconstructed systemic openness; if spirituality becomes more central, life-giving and prominent than before; or a renewed sense of gratitude begins to exist for the very breath of life, growth and beauty has occurred, and must not be diminished. This type of blooming needs to be meditated on, celebrated, and shared with trusted others, because it is not just a symbol of hope; but it is a reminder of the promise of resurrection that exists through the work of Jesus, for the loving sake of the world.

In addition, looming not only symbolize domains of change, but the color, hue, shape and contrast of the flowers also represent creative fruit which manifests to the world. Individually these blooming flowers of growth will look very different depending on each person's history, context, giftings, wounding and healing path. For example, personal strength might be the realization of how much courage it has taken one individual to communicate their story of trauma to others through poetry and spoken word, realizing the influence that such courage has on the world around them. That very same petal of strength might also be interpedently connected to another petal of growth in relationships; in this individual finding a loved one who can co-journey and celebrate their expressive voice with them.

In the moment of risking to share their pain with a trusted other—the relational system of a traumatized individual might become more open, and allow for improved bonds to others who are in an expanding network of safety. This not could grow the quality of relational connections, but simultaneously open up the opportunity for new experiences of thriving, journeying, trusting, celebrating and gratitude, that can come after the openness to safely share pain, mourn, grieve, and intentionally remember and narrate a traumatic experience. For some, this may actually be the discovery of a creative avenue in community, and for others—a creative modality—such as abstract oil painting, might demonstrate an entirely new form of communication, that is itself a manifestation of growth.

For another individual, the petal of spirituality may stand rekindled, as the sense of dependent connection on God, and perhaps increased in the face of a tragedy—that they are able to realize that the evils of the world can never conquer the love, and power of God. If this dependence contains a re-discovery of play as held in the unshakable love of God, an empowered spiritual purpose may result. A percussionist who reconnects, or is surprised by God's continual presence and purpose in their lives, even in the wake of tragedy, may find a level of passionate rhythms and syncopation, that synergize with spiritual courage and comfort.

Meanwhile, a petal of appreciation for the very breath of life, in a deeper recognition of the fragility, particularity and sanctity of the world alive around them. Many who survive a tragedy, can also simultaneous experience an increased level of gratitude for the life they have. Time becomes more valuable in a shaken worldview, and so does the fragility and beauty of life, especially if an individual has re-established a baseline of secure connection with others, and their own physiological responses. Though this experience is undoubtedly attached to feelings of loss and fear around traumatic experience, a re-awakened appreciation for life can birth a higher value on spontaneous play, and time spent in ways that are truly meaningful. A renewed, or newly discovered passion—such as watercolor painting, guitar, landscape photography, or expressive writing—can be a creative manifestation of appreciation for life.

The Holy Spirit: Nourishment, Sustenance, and Resurrection Power

Each part of the symbol of the desert rose—the root system, caudex, and flowering—ultimately derives nourishment and sustenance, through the overarching, and undergirding flow of life that exists through oxygenation. The Holy Spirit in particular, is the person of the Trinity known as the *paraclete* (helper, intercessor, counselor or advisor); and the breath or wind, of God (*ruach* in Hebrew, *pneuma* in Greek; Yong, 2010). The Holy Spirit is also the personal inhabitation of Jesus' resurrection power, living within God's children, and in many ways is like the breath and oxygen of life (Rom 8:11; Moltmann, 1992). Theologically the work of the Spirit is what breathes life into recovery, prepares and sustains growth, and connects God's children to the indwelling of Christ's victory over death. It is the breath of life, and the creative oxygen of God through whom "'we live and move and have our being'; and inhabits us as adopted sons and daughters of God, which Luke concludes speaking in respect to Greco-Roman culture, as "even some of your own poets have said, 'For we too are his offspring.'" (Acts 17:28 NRSV).

Concerning the desert rose, the Holy Spirit symbolically reflects the presence and need for oxygen, and the corresponding process of respiration.

Respiration is the process which enables photosynthesis—the ability of plants to use carbon dioxide and sunlight to produce growth and release back oxygen (Paul et al., 2016). Consequently, oxygen enables respiration which allows plants to photosynthesize, and release their own oxygen. Oxygen for plants and humans alike, is the *ruach*, wind, or breath of life, which the Spirit of God brings; this same Spirit which hovered over the chaos of the waters in *Genesis*, and is connected to the breath first breathed into Adam's lungs.

However, the Holy Spirit's movement—and paralleling presence and the release of oxygen—is often stirred within a community of people, perhaps as evidenced through movements such as the Azusa Street Revival, 1906–15. For the desert rose, this reflects the need not only for oxygen, but also for the collective involvement and synergy of the surrounding ecosystem. The Spirit's presence in the human ecosystem evidences the presence and power of Jesus—the loving, just, ever-faithful will of God that enables a furious grace, fidelity, healing, renewal and sustenance of authentic faith (Manning, 2009; Price, 2008). Just as Jesus states in Matt 18:19–20:

> Again, truly I tell you, if two of you agree on earth about anything you ask, it will be done for you by my Father in heaven. For where two or three are gathered in my name, I am there among them. (NRSV)

This is the relationally charged ecosystem of the coming kingdom in the incarnate presence of Christ's love on earth; in which play and creativity might become a collective expression Easter freedom, which is Christ's standing victory over sin, death, and Hades (Rev 1:17–18; Moltmann, 1992; Moltmann et al., 1972).

If a person or community is to empower play, liberation, vitality, perseverance, and growth in the wake of grief, adversity and traumatic fractures, genuine love must be present, and hope must break in: both of which are connected to the Spirit's work (Moltmann, 1992; Moltmann et al., 1972). And if dependence upon the work of the Spirit is the oxygen for the potential desert rose that abides within God's beloved, and enables the respiration of growth and hope, there must be an essential humility that surrounds the process of recovery. The humility of the communal, interpersonal and intimate solidarity prepares an individual for what Herman (1997) calls reconnection, which sets a basis for new growth to be sustained.

Paul reminds the church in 1 Cor 3:7–9 that it is "neither the one who plants nor the one who waters" who gives life "but [it is] only God who gives the growth. The one who plants and the one who waters have a common purpose. . . . For we are God's servants, working together; you are God's field, God's building" (Jewish Annotated New Testament). For clinicians, this is a humbling reminder of a power that is not our own, but is bestowed to cultivate and work in concert with the Spirit of God, who is the healing power within psychological, physiological, and spiritual change. The Spirit reveals Jesus in and alongside the vulnerable, while also consummating the present and ultimate hope in Christ, within the world. It is also God who, as Paul also states in Rom 8:28, causes "all things" (Greek, *panta*) to "work together" (*synergei*) for the good of God's beloved (NRSV; Osborne, 2004; Strong, 2003).

This type of humility, and dependence on the movements of God through the Spirit, may reflect part of Jesus' own quoting of Deuteronomy during his persecution in the desert wilderness. Jesus states that "One does not live by bread alone, but by every word that comes from the mouth of God" (Matt 4:4 Jewish Annotated New Testament). Just as a plant cannot operate, grow or release oxygen, without oxygen; humans from a theological perspective, cannot recover apart from the life, breadth and sustenance of the Holy Spirit, which Moltmann (1992) aptly refers to as the Spirit of Life. But the presence of hope in the Spirit, also entails the immanent reality of Christ's suffering before, within and along with traumatized people (Moltmann, 1974). For people to come to a place of play, creativity, and vitality; compassionate solidarity is the strength of the soil, which holds roots in place through the co-endurance of relationships, and fields of safety and understanding that provide sacred holding spaces.

This co-endurance, is empowered by Christ's own passion that is at once completed, and continues with and among us (Moltmann, 1974). Safe harbor for the wounded and broken; the ability to derive sustenance during honest, painful emotional processing; and the budding flower petals that glisten of hope that in the midst of tragedy, are all processes in which the Holy Spirit is present; the incarnate and resurrected Jesus abides as a "tender shoot" (Isa 53:2), in our suffering as "broken reed[s]" (Isa 42:3; Matt 12:20). Isaiah 53:2–5 prophetically describes Jesus, the suffering servant, Immanuel, God with us:

> For He grew up before Him like a tender shoot, and like a root out of parched ground; He has no stately form or majesty that we should look upon Him, nor appearance that we should be attracted to Him. He was despised and forsaken of men, a man

of sorrows and acquainted with grief; And like one from whom men hide their face he was despised, and we did not esteem Him. Surely our griefs He Himself bore, and our sorrows He carried; Yet we ourselves esteemed Him stricken (struck down) by God, and afflicted. But He was pierced through for our transgressions, He was crushed for our iniquities; The chastening for our well-being fell upon Him, and by His scourging we are healed. (NASB)

CONCLUSION

Christians may be familiar with the theological implications of the scripture of Isaiah, but it may help to intentionally soak in it. In doing so we might store the truth of Isaiah's prophecy of what was, is and continues to be the work of Christ on the earth, by the Spirit, through the church, in the midst of the spiritually, emotionally and physically poor, marginalized, weak, desperate, hurting, hungry, disillusioned, seeking of humanity. As Howard Thurman (1949) describes Jesus gives full inheritance to the disinherited. Jesus restores the play, creativity and imagination of childhood to the traumatized, afflicted, and disregarded. God's mysterious, but powerful presence among the vulnerable, afflicted, and weak is evident in the Sermon on the Mount (Matthew 5), in which the blessing of the kingdom (known as the Beatitudes) rests upon those who experience persecution, are impoverished in spirit, mourn, hunger for righteousness, seek peace and demonstrate purity. Within the Beatitudes is a sacred identification with the caustic pain of living in a broken world, but also for the genuine hunger for pure love, just action, and renewed spirit that is stirred beneath the surface of affliction. This liberation is what allows the true self to flourish, as both Winnicott (1971) and Merton (1961) describe from their respective disciplines and tradition, and enables movement of childlike trust that undergirds the fullness of being, and genuine creative expression (Manning, 2009; Moltmann, 1992).

Jesus later states in Matthew 18:3, "Truly I tell you, unless you change and become like children, you will never enter the kingdom of heaven." There are many angles from which a person or community can interpret Jesus' words; and from a Winnicottian viewpoint, the reader might especially resonate with childlikeness as the "true self," the ability to play, to feel joy, to engage, to explore, create and to love in the freedom of God's unconditional, trustworthy, and ever-fervent love. From the standpoint of trauma, this might even prompt the sacred engagement with simultaneous mourning, hunger for justice, longing for restoration and need for creative communication that aches within a trauma survivor. These feelings are God-given, and should not be suppressed in one's network of safety. They must be engaged with, and from this sacred space, unexpected transformation may occur—whether that is in days, weeks, years, or generations. They are the roots that might grow to increasing depths into kingdom soil, despite the immediacy of circumstances. Further, it is not a solitary work, but a community, as Herman (1997) describes which can powerfully bear witness. In the book of Matthew, very soon after Jesus states that the kingdom of heaven is received in childlike—perhaps, authentic, vulnerable, spontaneously trusting—posture, he also says:

> Truly I tell you, whatever you bind on earth will be bound in heaven, and whatever you loose on earth will be loosed in heaven. Again, truly I tell you, if two of you agree on earth about anything you ask, it will be done for you by my Father in heaven. For where two or three are gathered in my name, I am there among them. (Matt 18:18–20 NRSV)

Gale (2011) comments that Jewish law would require two or three individuals to constitute a substantive witness. Bearing witness to trauma, witness to the story, and witness to hope in love are communal actions which Jesus is incarnate, and powerfully present within (Jones, 2010). The good news of the Beatitudes is bound on earth as it is in heaven through relationships that open and vulnerably present the reality and hunger of life.

The sense of the Beatitudes living within the core of a trauma survivor must be treated with reverent, tender care, in the full systemic perspective of a person's livelihood. The desert rose, preaches the Beatitudes through creative emergence, as the St. Francis likely would have understood (Rohr, 2014). This is the foundation for the adenium of the heart to root and return to a place of nourishment, and as God spoke through the prophet Isaiah (30:15) "In returning and rest you shall be saved; in quietness and in trust shall be your strength." There is a sacred need for holding space, a place for childlike self to return and trust, for the self whom God has made us to become even in the face of persecution and mourning—so that we may adorn the humble gateway to kingdom life, and participate with God's very life present on earth. Paul, describing the freedom that comes from the new life found in Christ, instructs believers to "Let your roots grow down into him, and let your lives be built on him. Then your faith will grow strong in the truth you were taught, and you will overflow with thankfulness" (Col 2:7 NLT). The root system, which has been described as the sacred holding space for survivors of trauma, caudex of creative and meaningful experiences, and flowering of expressive growth, draws life from the very life of God, and the unconditional love of Christ, who fulfills the original design of God and the redemptive work of history, into the immediate, cosmic, eternal significance (Moltmann, 1992).

So as clinicians, psychologists, and the ecumenical the church community continue to engage and share in the inevitable disorientation, fear and pain caused by trauma; we must also recognize dependence on the Spirit of God to do the work of growth before us, even if we cannot seed of the desert rose are yet to visibly break through the soil, let alone blossom. But the work of creating, cultivating, shaping and stewarding the earth and its resources is also a process of being God's beloved. This process is held by the creative oxygenating of the Holy Spirit, a *ruach* which hovers over the chaos of liminal forms before beauty and goodness begins to manifest, as described in Genesis. Christ fulfills history and can transform tragedy into hope for the oppressed and afflicted; who are peoples with whom God's incarnate compassion rests (Moltmann, 1974; Moltmann, 1992; Moltmann, 1996).

Isaiah prophetically declared that "a bruised reed he [God]will not break, and a faintly burning wick he will not quench; he will faithfully bring forth justice" (Isa 42:3; Matt 12:20 NLT). The community of faith must hold onto this promise for the acutely, chronically, and communally traumatized, knowing the Spirit moves and sustains the life of the vulnerable; which is revealed in the person and work of Jesus Christ by his life, death, resurrection and ascension (John 14:6; 1 John 2:1). The Love of the Father in process, empowering the people of God, bearing all thing, enduring all things, hopes all things, and believing in all things (1 Cor 13:7 NRSV). The love of the Father, the Son, and the Holy Spirit go before us, and this process of restoration is not dependent on our performance as, but exists within our imperfect processes. The road to recovery, and restoration of creative vitality may be riddled with pain, complexity, confusion and failures to embrace forgiveness, hope and love. Fortunately, the church's precedent for the Spirit's movement and cohabitation of Christ within us, is not based upon our performance (Price, 2008). Peter may be the example for many of us. Impatient, fervent, and denying Jesus multiple times in the most critical of hours, and, consequently denying his true self, attached to Christ, who is the attached source of unconditional love, truth and life. Yet, it is still Peter whom Jesus gives the keys of the kingdom—perhaps the ultimate spiritual transitional object—that unlocks the incarnate inbreaking body of hope, which is the church. The life of Peter might speak truth for each person's creative endeavors, and the creative endeavors of church as a whole, out of trauma and into reclaimed living.

When Jesus affirms, "You are Peter (*Petros*), and on this rock (*petra*) I will build my church, and the gates of Hades will not prevail against it" (Matt 16:18 Jewish Annotated New Testament), Jesus breaks preconceptions of performance-based worth, and the very power of death; as the keys are not given to the one who is the most spiritually steadfast, but to one who was initially grieved by his own impulsivity, misunderstanding and cowardice. One might imagine that this cherished experience filled Peter with an irrational joy, and brought the childlike ability to dream, create, play, and love back into connection, so that the Good News may find its way into every corner of the earth. Through participation in the process of recovery and even growth with the traumatized, the church participates in the Spirit's work of healing, restoration and the hope of fullness. As individuals and communities facilitate a rest, and a return to a place of childlike play and creative expression; the community may all, learn to play, hope, endure, forgive and love in the fullness of who each person was created to become, as adopted sons and daughters of God, and co-heirs with Christ, who is with us in our suffering, our liminality and transitional experiences, our spontaneous joy, and our resurrection power with, and in Christ (Gal 3:26; 4:5–7; Rom 8:14–23; 9:8). Those who create from this sacred place preach the hope of Christ in the spontaneity of trust, while sharing from the depths of what it means to be made in the image of God. The arts, media, communal creativity, and playful generativity are no longer pastimes, but become a holy participation that brings glory to the work and presence of Christ within us, the Spirit among us, and the Father's love upon us.

Figures

Figure 1. *Adenium Obesum* (Waddington, 2015).

Figure 2. *Adenium Obesum* Species (Waddington, 2017).

Figure 3. *Adenium Obesum* Caudex (Waddington, 2019).

Figure 4. *Adenium Obesum* Petals (Simon, 2013).

References

Adams, H. L. (2015). Insights into processes of posttraumatic growth through narrative analysis of chronic illness stories. *Qualitative Psychology*, 2, 111–29. doi:10.1037/qupo000025.

Adenauer, H., Catani, C., Gola, H., Keil, J., Ruf, M., Schauer M., & Neuner, F. (2011). Narrative exposure therapy for PTSD increases top-down processing of aversive stimuli—evidence from a randomized controlled treatment trial. *BMC Neuroscience*, 127, doi:10.1186/1471-2202-12-127.

Afari, N., Ahumada, S. M., Wright, L. J., Mostoufi, S., Golnari, G., Reis, V., & Cuneo, J. G. (2014). Psychological trauma and functional somatic syndromes: A systematic review and meta-analysis. *Psychosomatic Medicine*, 76, 2–11. doi:10.1097/PSY.0000000000000010.

Alschuler, M. (2006). Poetry, the healing pen. In S. L. Brooke (Ed.), *Creative arts therapies manual* (pp. 253–62). Charles C. Thomas.

American Music Therapy Association. (2011). Music therapy as crisis project intervention with survivors of the attacks on the World Trade Centers in New York City, September 11, 2001. In B. Hesser & H. N. Heinemann (Eds.), *Music as a global resource: Solutions for social and economic issues* (pp. 139–40). United Nations.

American Psychiatric Association. (2013). *Diagnostic and statistical manual of mental disorders* (5th ed.). American Psychiatric Association.

Avrhami, D. (2006). Visual art therapy's unique contribution in the treatment of posttraumatic stress disorders. *Journal of Trauma and Dissociation*, 6, 5–38. doi:10.1300/J229v06n04_02.

Baker, J. M., Kelly, C., Calhoun, L. G., Cann, A., & Tedeschi, R. G. (2008). An examination of posttraumatic growth and depreciation: Two exploratory studies. *Journal of Loss and Trauma*, 13, 450–65.

Balswick, J. O., Reimer, K. S., & King, P. E. (2005). *The reciprocating self: Human development in psychological perspective*. InterVarsity Press.

Bass, M., DeDreu, C. K. W. & Nijstad, B. (2008). A meta-analysis of 25 years of mood-creativity research: Hedonic tone, activation, or regulatory focus? *Psychological Bulletin*, 134, 779–806. http://dx.doi.org/10.1037/a0012815.

Beck, R. (2012). *The authenticity of faith: The varieties and illusions of religious experience*. Abilene Christian University Press.

Bellizzi, K. M., & Blank, T. O. (2006). Predicting posttraumatic growth in breast cancer survivors. *Health Psychology*, 25, 47–56. doi:10.1037/0278-6133.25.1.47.

References

BenEzer, G. (2012). From Winnicott's potential space to mutual creative space: A principle for intercultural psychotherapy. *Transcultural Psychiatry, 49*, 323–39. doi:10.1177/1363461511435803.

Benner, J. A. (2019). *Hebrew word definitions: Soul.* Ancient Hebrew Research Center. http://www.ancient-hebrew.org/vocabulary_definitions_soul.html.

Bensimon, M., Amir, D., & Wolf, Y. (2012). A pendulum between trauma and life: Group music therapy with post-traumatized soldiers. *The Arts in Psychotherapy, 39*, 223–33. doi:10.1016/j.aip.2012.03.005.

Berry, W. (2009). *The selected poems of Wendell Berry.* Counterpoint.

Bethel Redding. (2019). *Creative arts.* http://www.bethelredding.com/content/creative-arts.

Bland, E. D., & Strawn, B. D. (2014). A new conversation. In E. D. Bland & B. D. Strawn (Eds.), *Christianity and psychoanalysis: A new conversation* (pp. 13–37). InterVarsity Press.

Blom, R. (2004). *The handbook of Gestalt play therapy: Practical guidelines for child therapists.* Kingsley.

Bodrova, E., Gemeroth, C., & Leong, D. J. (2013). Play and self-regulation: Lessons from Vygotzky. *American Journal of Play, 6*, 111–23.

Bonaminio, V., & DiRenzo, M. (2000). Creativity, playing, dreaming: Overlapping circles in the work of Marion Milner and D. W. Winnicott. In L. Caldwell (Ed.), *Art, creativity, living* (pp. 97–112). Karnac Books & The Squiggle Foundation.

Bowlby, J. (1969). *Attachment and loss, Vol. 1: Attachment.* Basic Books.

Bradt, J. (2006). The history of music therapy. In S. L. Brooke (Ed.), *Creative arts therapies manual* (pp. 168–74). Charles C. Thomas.

Brady, K. T., Back, S. E., & Coffey, S. F. (2004). Substance abuse and posttraumatic stress disorder. *Current Directions in Psychological Science, 13*, 206–9. doi:10.1111/j.0963-7214.2004.00309.x.

Breslau, N., Chilcoat, H. D., Kessler, R. C., & Davis, G. C. (1999). Previous exposure to trauma and PTSD effects of subsequent trauma: results from the Detroit Area Survey of trauma. *American Journal of Psychiatry, 156*, 902–7. doi: 10.1176/ajp.156.6.902.

Briere, J. (2004). Trauma types and characteristics. In J. Briere (Ed.), *Psychological assessment of adult posttraumatic states: Phenomenology, diagnosis, and measurement* (pp. 5–37). American Psychological Association.

Brown, W. S. (2004). Resonance: A model for relating science, psychology and faith. *Journal of Psychology and Christianity, 23*, 110–20.

Brueggemann, W. (1982). *Genesis.* Interpretation. John Knox.

Brueggemann, W. (2001). *The prophetic imagination* (2nd ed.). Fortress.

Calhoun, L. G., & Tedeschi, R. G. (1998). Posttraumatic growth: Future directions. In R. G. Tedeschi, C. L. Park, & L. G. Calhoun (Eds.), *Posttraumatic growth: Positive changes in the aftermath of crisis* (pp. 215–38). Erlbaum.

Calhoun, L. G., & Tedeschi, R. G. (2006). The foundations of posttraumatic growth: An expanded framework. In L. G. Calhoun & R. G. Tedeschi (Eds.), *Handbook of post traumatic growth: Research and practice* (pp. 3–23). Erlbaum.

Calhoun, L. G., & Tedeschi, R. G. (2013). *Posttraumatic growth in clinical practice.* Routledge.

Campbell, M., Decker, K. P., Kruk, K., & Deaver, S. P. (2016). Art therapy and cognitive processing therapy for combat-related PTSD: A randomized controlled trial. *Journal for the American Art Therapy Association, 4*, 169–77. doi:10.1080/07421656.2016.1 226643.

Cann, A., Calhoun, L. G., Tedeschi, R. G., & Solomon, D. T. (2010). Posttraumatic growth and depreciation as independent experiences and predictors of well-being. *Journal of Loss and Trauma, 15*, 151–66. doi:10.10808/15325020903375826.

Cann, A., Calhoun, L. G., Tedeschi, R. G., Triplett, K. N., Vishnevsky, T., & Lindstrom, T. M. (2011). Assessing posttraumatic cognitive processes: The event related rumination inventory. *Anxiety, Stress, & Coping, 24*, 137–56.

Carr, C., d'Ardenne, P., Sloboda, A., Scott, C., Wang, D., & Priebe, S. (2011). Group music therapy for patients with persistent post-traumatic stress disorder—An exploratory randomized controlled trial with mixed methods evaluation. *Psychology and Psychotherapy, 85*, 179–202. doi:10.1111/j.2044-8351.2011.02026.x.

Carroll, R. (2005). Finding the words to say it: The healing power of poetry. *Evidence Based Complementary Medicine, 2*, 161–72. doi:10.1093/ecam/neho96.

Chilton, G. (2013). Art therapy and flow: A review of the literature and applications. *Art Therapy: Journal of the American Art Therapy Association, 30*, 64–70. doi:10.1080/0 7421656.2013.787211.

Collignon, O., Dormal, G., Albouy, G., Vandewalle, G., Voss, P., Phillips, C., & Lepore, F. (2013). Impact of blindness onset on functional organization and the connectivity of the occipital cortex. *Brain, 136*, 2769–83. https://doi.org/10.1093/brain/awt176.

Cooke, G. (2010). *Prophetic wisdom*. Brilliant House.

Connor, K. M. (2006). Assessment of resilience in the aftermath of trauma. *Journal of Clinical Psychiatry, 67*, 46–49.

Courtois, C. A., & Ford, J. D. (2009). Defining and understanding complex trauma and complex traumatic stress disorders. In C. A. Courtois and J. D. Ford (Eds.), *Treating complex traumatic stress disorders: An evidence-based guide* (pp. 13–30). Guilford.

Cozolino, L. (2010). *The neuroscience of psychotherapy: Healing the social brain* (2nd ed.). Norton.

Crenshaw, D. (2006). Neuroscience and trauma treatment: Implications for creative art therapists. In L. Carey (Ed.), *Expressive and creative art methods for trauma survivors* (pp. 21–33). Kingsley.

Csikszentmihalyi, M. (1996). *Creativity: Flow and the psychology of discovery and invention*. Harper Perennial.

Danhauer, S. C., Russel, G. B., Tedeschi, R. G., Jesse, M. T., Vishnevsky, T., Daley, K., Carroll, S., Triplett, K. N., Calhoun, L. G., Cann, A., & Powell, B. L. (2013). A longitudinal investigation of post traumatic growth in adult patients undergoing treatment for acute leukemia. *Journal of Clinical Psychology in Medical Settings, 20*, 13–24. doi:10.1007/s10880-012-9304-5.

Danvers, A. F., & Shiota, M. N. (2017). Going off script: Effects of awe on memory for script-typical and irrelevant narrative detail. *Emotion, 17*, 938–52. doi:10/1037/ emo0000277.

Dieterich-Hartwell, R. (2017). Dance/movement therapy in the treatment of posttraumatic stress disorder: A reference model. *The Arts in Psychotherapy, 54*, 38–46. doi:10.1016/j.aip.2017.02.010.

Dimmit, M. A. (1997). *How plants cope with the desert climate*. Arizona-Sonora Desert Museum. www.desertmuseum.org/programs/succulents_adaptation.php.

Dimmit, M. A., Joseph, G. E., & Palzkill, D. A. (2009). *Adenium: sculptural elegance, floral extravagance*. Scathingly Brilliant Idea.

References

Elliott, D. M. (1997). Traumatic events: Prevalence and delayed recall in general population. *Journal of Consulting and Clinical Psychology, 65,* 811–20. http://dx.doi.org/10.1037/0022-006X.65.5.811.

Fenson, L., Kagan, J., Kearsley, R. B., & Zelazo, P. R. (1976). The developmental progression of manipulative play in the first two years. *Child Development, 47,* 232–36. doi:10.2307/1128304.

Fisher, E. P. (1992). The impact of play on development: A meta-analysis. *Play and Culture, 5,* 159–81.

Forgeard, M. J. C. (2013). Perceiving benefits after adversity: The relationship between self-reported post traumatic growth and creativity. *Psychology of Aesthetics, Creativity, and the Arts, 7,* 245–64. doi:10.1037/a0031223.

Fosha, D. (2003). Dyadic regulation and experiential work with emotional and relatedness in trauma and disorganized attachment. In M. F. Solomon & D. J. Siegel (Eds.), *Healing trauma: Attachment, mind, body and brain* (pp. 221–82). Norton.

Fosha, D. (2009). Emotion and cognition at work: Energy, vitality, pleasure, truth and the emergent phenomenology of transformational experience. In D. Fosha, D. J. Siegel, & M. Solomon (Eds.), *The healing power of emotion: Affective neuroscience, development, and clinical practice* (pp. 172–203). Norton.

Frankl, V. (2006). *Man's search for meaning.* Beacon.

Fratarolli, J. (2006). Experimental disclosure and its moderators: A meta-analysis. *Psychological Bulletin, 6,* 823–65.

Gale, A. M. (2011). Matthew. In A. Levine and M. Brettler (Eds.), *The Jewish annotated new testament* (pp. 1–54). Oxford University Press.

Gallegos, R. A., & Hillbrand, M. (2016). Integrative treatment of complex trauma: Integrating behavioral, dynamic, and attribution models. *Journal of Psychotherapy Integration, 26,* 259–72. http://dx.doi.org/10.1037/a0040043.

Gant, L., & Tripp, T. (2016). The image comes first: Treating preverbal trauma with art therapy. In J. King (Ed.), *Art therapy, trauma and neuroscience: Theoretical and practical perspectives* (pp. 67–99). Kingsley.

Gard, T., Noggle, J. J., Park, C. L., Vago, D. R., & Wilson, A. (2014). Potential self-regulatory mechanisms of yoga for psychological health. *Frontiers in Human Neuroscience, 8,* 770. doi:10.3389/fnhum.2014.00770.

Garland, S. N., Carlson, L. E., Cook, S., Lansdell, S., & Speca, M. (2007). A non-randomized comparison of mindfulness-based stress reduction and healing arts programs for facilitating posttraumatic growth and spirituality in cancer outpatients. *Supportive Care in Cancer, 15,* 949–61. doi:10.1007/s00520-007-0280-5.

Garrido, S., Baker, F. A., Davidson, J. W., Moore, G., & Wasserman, S. (2015). Music and trauma: The relationship between music, personality and coping style. *Frontiers in Psychology, 6,* 977. doi:10.3389/fpsyg.2015.00977.

Gilbert, R. M. (2006). *The eight concepts of Bowen theory: A new way of thinking about the individual and the group.* Leading Systems Press.

Gold, C., Voracek, M., & Wigram, T. (2004). Effects of music therapy for children and adolescents with psychopathology: A meta-analysis. *Journal of Child Psychology and Psychiatry, 45,* 1054–63. doi:10.1111/j.1469-7610.2004.t01-1-00298.x.

Goldingay, J. (2003). *Old testament theology, vol. 1: Israel's gospel.* InterVarsity Press.

Gonzales, J. L. (1996). *Santa Biblia: The Bible through Hispanic eyes.* Abingdon.

Gonzales, J. L. (2010). *The story of Christianity, vol. 1: The early church to the dawn of the reformation.* HarperCollins.

Grolnick, S. A. (1990). *The work and pay of Winnicott*. Jason Aronson, Inc.

Guilford, J. P. (1950). Creativity. *American 'Psychologist, 5*, 444–54. http://dx.doi.org/10.1037/h0063487.

Hass-Cohen, N. (2008). CREATE: Art therapy relational neuroscience principles (ATR-N). In N. Hass-Cohen & R. Carr (Eds.), *Art therapy and clinical neuroscience* (pp. 283–309). Jessica Kingsley Publishers.

Hass-Cohen, N. (2016). Secure resiliency. In J. King (Ed.), *Art therapy, trauma, and neuroscience: Theoretical and practical perspectives* (pp. 100–138). Jessica Kingsley Publishers.

Hass-Cohen, N. & Findlay, J. C. (2015). *Art therapy and the neuroscience of relationships, creativity and resiliency: Skills and practices*. W. W. Norton & Company.

Hectorne, S. M. (2017). *Peace paper project* [Conference presentation]. HMS Schools Peace Studies 2018, Hudson Mentessori School, Hudson, Ohio.

Hennesey, B. A., & Amabile, T. M. (2010). Creativity. *Annual Review Psychology, 61*, 569–98. doi:10.1146/annurev.psych.093008.100416.

Herman, J. (1997). *Trauma and recovery: The aftermath of violence—From domestic abuse to political terror*. Basic Books.

Hoekema, A. A. (1986). *Created in God's image*. Eerdmans.

Hoffman, J., & Russ, S. W. (2012). Pretend play, creativity, and emotional regulation in children. *Psychology of Creativity, and the Arts, 6*, 175–84. doi:10.1037/a0026299.

Hoffman, M. T. (2011). *Toward mutual recognition: Relational psychoanalysis and the Christian narrative*. Routledge.

Hollingsworth, A. (2011). *Holy curiosity: Cultivating the creative spirit in everyday life*. Cascade Books.

Holmes, R. M., Romeo, L., Ciraola, S., & Grushko, M. (2015). The relationship between creativity, social play, and children's language abilities. *Early Childhood Development and Care, 185*, 1180–97. doi:10.1037/t15144-000.

Howes, C., & Matheson, C. C. (1992). Sequences in the development of competent play with peers: Social and social pretend play. *Developmental Psychology, 28*, 961–74. doi:10.1037/0012-1649.28.5.961.

Janoff-Bulman, R. (1992). *Shattered assumptions*. Free Press.

Janoff-Bulman, R. (2006). Schema-change perspectives on posttraumatic growth. In L. G. Calhoun & R. G. Tedeschi (Eds.), *Handbook for posttraumatic growth* (pp. 81–98). Taylor & Francis.

Johnson, D. R. (1987). The role of the creative arts therapies in the diagnosis and treatment of psychological trauma. *The Arts in Psychotherapy, 14*, 7–13.

Johnson, D. R., Lahad, M., & Gray, A. (2009). Creative therapies for adults. In E. B. Foa, T. M. Keane, M. J. Friedman, & J. A. Cohen (Eds.), *Effective treatments for PTSD: Practice guidelines from the international society for traumatic stress studies* (pp. 479–91). Guilford.

Johnson, S. M. (2004). *The practice of emotionally focused couple therapy: Creating connection*. Routledge.

Johnston, R. K. (1983). *The Christian at play*. Eerdmans.

Johnston, R. K. (2014). *God's wider presence: Reconsidering general revelation*. Baker Academic.

Jones, D. R. (2010). *The two sides of posttraumatic growth: A study of the Janus face model in a college population*. Proquest LLC.

Jones, S. (2010). *Trauma and grace: Theology in a ruptured world*. Westminster John Knox.

References

Kahr, B. (2004). Introduction of Sir Richard Bowlby, John Bowlby and Donald Winnicott: Collegial comrades in mental health. In P. King (Ed.), *Fifty years of attachment theory: The Donald Winnicott memorial lecture* (pp. 3–11). Karnac.

Kapitan, L., Litell, M., & Torres, A. (2011). Creative art therapy in a community's participatory research and social transformation. *Art Therapy: Journal of the American Art Therapy Association, 28*, 64–73. doi:10.1080/07421656.2011.578238.

Karen, R. (1998). *Becoming attached: First relationships and how they shape our capacity to love.* Oxford University Press.

Kärkkäinen, V. M. (2002). *Pneumatology: The Holy Spirit in ecumenical, international, and contextual perspective.* Baker Academic.

Kärkkäinen, V. M. (2016). *Christology: A global introduction.* Baker Academic.

Kaufman, S. B., & Gregoire, C. (2015). *Wired to create: Unraveling the mysteries of the creative mind.* TarcherPerigee.

Kelley, W. M., Mccrae, C. N., Wyland, C. L., Caglar, S., Inati, S., & Heatherton, T. F. (2002). Finding the self? An event-related fMRI study. *Journal of Cognitive Neuroscience, 14*, 785–94. doi:10.1162/08989290260138672.

Kessler, R. C., Sonnega, A., Bromet, E., Hughes, M., & Nelson, C. B. (1995). Posttraumatic stress disorder in the National Comorbidity Study. *Archives of General Psychiatry, 52*, 1048 –1060. doi:10.1001/archpsyc.1995.03950240066012.

Kessler, R. C., Sonnega, A., Bromet, E., Hughes, M., Nelson, C. B., & Breslau, N. (1999). Epidemiological risk factors for trauma and PTSD. In R. Yehuda (Ed.), *Risk factors for posttraumatic stress disorder* (pp. 23–59). American Psychiatric Association.

King, J. (2016). Introduction. In J. King (Ed.), *Art therapy, trauma and neuroscience: Theoretical and practical perspectives* (pp. 1–10). Kingsley.

Klorer, P. G. (2016). Neuroscience and art therapy with severely traumatized children. In J. King (Ed.), *Art therapy, trauma and neuroscience* (pp. 139–56). Routledge.

Konopka, L. M. (2015). Neuroscience concepts in clinical practice. In J. King (Ed.), *Art therapy, trauma and neuroscience* (pp. 9–41). Routledge.

Koss, J. D., & Trantham, S. M. (2013). Perspectives from clinical neuroscience: Mindfulness and the therapeutic use of the arts. In L. Rappaport (Ed.), *Mindfulness and the creative art therapies.* Kinglsey.

Lamb, D. (2011). *God behaving badly: Is the God of the Old Testament angry, racist and sexist?* InterVarsity Press.

Larsen, S. E., & Berenbaum, H. (2015). Are specific emotional regulation strategies differentially associated with posttraumatic growth versus posstraumatic stress? *Treatment Strategies for Traumatic Events, 794*–808. doi:10.1080/10926771.2015.10 62451.

LaVerdiere, E. M. (2006). Music therapy theoretical approaches. In S. L. Brooke (Ed.), *Creative arts therapies manual* (pp. 175–81). Charles C. Thomas.

Lazarus, R. A. (1999). *Stress and emotion: A new synthesis.* Spring Publishing.

Lee, S. (2013). "Flow" in art therapy: Empowering immigrant children with adjustment difficulties. *Art Therapy: Journal of the American Art Therapy Association, 30*, 56–63. doi:10.1080/07421656.2013.786978.

Lee, S. W., Gerdes, L., Tegeler, C. L., Shaltout, H. A., & Tegeler, C. H. (2014). A bihemispheric autonomic model for traumatic stress effects on health and behavior. *Frontiers Psychology, 5*, 843. doi:10.3389/fpsyg.2014.00843.

Levine, B., & Land, H. M. (2016). A meta-synthesis of qualitative findings about dance/movement therapy for individuals with trauma. *Qualitative Health Research, 26,* 330–34. doi:10.1177/1049732315589920.

Levine, P. A., & Frederick, A. (1997). *Waking the tiger: Healing trauma.* North Atlantic.

Lillard, A. S., Lerner, M. D., Hopkins, E. J., Dore, R. A., Smith, E. D., & Palmquist, C. M. (2013). The impact of pretend play on children's development: A review of the evidence. *Psychological Bulletin, 139,* 1–34. doi:10.1037/a0029321.

Linley, P. A., Felus, A., Gillett, R., & Joseph, S. (2011). Emotional expression and growth following adversity: Emotional expression mediates subjective distress and is moderated by emotional intelligence. *Journal of Loss and Trauma, 16,* 387–401. doi: 10.1080/15325024.2011.572036.

Linley, P. A., & Joseph, S. (2004). Positive change following trauma and adversity: A review. *Journal of Traumatic Stress, 17*(1), 11–21.

Louth, A. (2012). Apophatic and cataphatic theology. In A. M. Hollywood & P. Z. Beckham (Eds.), *Cambridge companion to Christian mysticism* (pp. 137–46). Oxford University Press.

Lusebrink, V. J., & Hinz, L. D. (2016). The expressive therapies continuum as a framework in the treatment of trauma. In J. L. King (Ed.), *Art therapy, trauma and neuroscience: Theoretical and practical perspectives* (pp. 42–66). Routledge.

Maercker, A., & Zoellner, T. (2004). The Janus face of self-perceived growth: Toward a two-component model of posttraumatic growth. *Psychological Inquiry, 15*(1), 41–48.

Magnuson, C. D., & Barnett, L. A. (2013). The playful advantage: How playfulness enhances coping with stress. *Leisure Sciences, 35,* 129–44.

Malchiodi, C. A., & Crenshaw, D. A. (Eds.). (2013). *Creative arts and play therapy for attachment problems.* Guildford.

Manning, B. (2009). *The furious longing of God.* David C. Cook.

Matott, D., & Miller, G. (2016). *Papermaking as social action and trauma intervention* [Conference presentation]. Papermaking as Social Action and Trauma Intervention, Ursuline College, Pepper Pike, Ohio.

Maulik, P. K., & Darmstadt, G. L. (2009). Community-based interventions to optimize early childhood development in low resource settings. *Journal of Perinatology, 29,* 531–42. doi:10.1038/jp.2009.42.

Mayo, K. R. (2009). *Creativity, spirituality and mental health: Exploring connections.* Ashgate Publishing.

McCauley, J. L., Killeen, T., Gros, D. F., Brady, K. T., & Back, S. E. (2012). Posttraumatic stress disorder and co-occurring substance abuse disorder: Advances in assessment and treatment. *Clinical Psychology, 19,* doi:10.1111/cpsp.12006.

Merton, T. (1961). *New seeds of contemplation.* New Directions.

Milner, M. (1957). *On not being able to paint.* Routledge.

Mitchell, S. A., & Black, M. J. (1995). *Freud and beyond: A history of modern psychoanalytic thought.* Basic Books.

Modell, A. H. (1976). "The holding environment" and the therapeutic action of psychoanalysis. *Journal of American Psychoanalytic Association, 24,* 285–307. doi:10.1177/000306517602400202.

Moltmann, J. (1974). *The crucified God.* Fortress.

Moltmann, J. (1992). *The spirit of life: A universal affirmation.* Fortress.

Moltmann, J. (1996). *The coming of God: Christian eschatology.* Fortress.

Moltmann, J. (2015). *The living god and the fullness of life.* Westminster John Knox.

Moltmann, J., Neale, R. E., Keen, S., & Miller, D. L. (1972). *Theology of play*. Harper & Row.

Moore, S. A., Zoellner, L. A., & Mollenholt N. (2008). Are expressive suppression and cognitive reappraisal associated with stress related symptoms? *Behaviour Research and Therapy, 46*, 993–1000. doi:10.1016/j.brat.2008.05.001.

Morris, B. A., Shakespeare-Finch, J., Rieck, M., & Newbery, J. (2005). Multidimensional nature of posttraumatic growth in an Australian population. *Journal of Traumatic Stress, 18*, 575–85. doi:10.1002/jts.20067.

Morris-Kay, G. M. (2010). The evolution of human artistic creativity. *Journal of Anatomy, 216*, 158–76. doi:10.1111/j.1469-7580.2009.01160.x.

Mullan, M. R. (1984). Motor development in children's play. In T. D. Yawkey & A. D. Pellegrini (Eds.), *Children's play and play therapy* (pp. 7–15). Technomic.

Müller, V., & Lindenberger, U. (2011). Cardiac and respiratory patterns synchronize between persons during choir singing. *PLoS ONE, 6*, doi:10.1371/journal.pone.0024893.

Murray, T. (2016). A sense of wonder: Why every creative writer needs one. In J. Oluwakemi, T. Murray & C. Boden-McGill (Eds.), *Enhancing Writing Skills* (pp. 59–64). Information Age.

Music, G. (2015). Bringing up the bodies: Psyche-soma, body awareness, and feeling at ease. *British Journal of Psychotherapy, 31*, 4–19.

Nakamura J., & Csikszentmihalyi, M. (2009). Flow theory and research. In C. R. Snyder & S. J. Lopez (Eds.), *Handbook of Positive Psychology* (pp. 195–206). Oxford University Press.

Negus, K., & Pickering, M. (2002). Creativity and musical experience. In D. Hesmondalgh, & K. Negus (Eds.), *Popular music studies* (pp. 178–90). Hodder Education.

Nemetz, L. D. (2006). Moving with meaning: The historical progression of dance/movement therapy. In S. L. Brooke (Ed.), *Creative arts therapies manual* (pp. 175–81). Charles C. Thomas.

Neuner, F., Schauer, M., Klaschik, C., Karunakara, U., & Elbert, T. (2004). A comparison of Narrative Exposure Therapy, supportive counseling, and psychoeducation for treating posttraumatic stress disorder in an African refugee settlement. *Journal of Consulting and Clinical Psychology, 72*, 579–87. doi: 10.1037/0022-006X.72.4.579.

Norris, F. H. (1992). Epidemiology of trauma: Frequency and impact of potentially traumatic events on different demographic groups. *Journal of Consulting and Clinical Psychology, 60*, 409–18. doi:10.1037//0022-006x.60.3.409.

Nouwen, H. (1997). *The wounded healer: Ministry in contemporary society*. Doubleday.

Ogden, P., Minton, K., & Pain, C. (2006). *Trauma and the body: A sensorimotor approach*. Norton.

Osborne, G. R. (2004). *Romans*. IVP Academic.

Ouimette, P. C., Brown, P. J., & Najavits, L. M. (1998). Course and treatment of patients with both substance use and posttraumatic stress disorders. *Addictive Behaviors, 23*, 785–95. doi:10.1016/S0306-4603(98)00064-1.

Outeiral, J. (2013). Living creatively: The concept of the sound-minded individual in the healing phenomena. In G. Goldstein (Ed.), *Art in psychoanalysis* (pp. 139–50). Karnac Books.

Park, C. L., Currier, J. M., Harris, J. I., & Slattery, J. M. (2017). *Trauma, meaning and spirituality: Translating research into clinical practice*. American Psychological Association. doi:10.1037/15961-000.

Parker, S. E. (1996). *Led by the spirit: Toward a practical theology of Pentecostal discernment and decision making.* Sheffield Academic.

Parker, S. E. (2011). *Winnicott and religion.* Aronson.

Paul, D., Biswas, K., & Narayan Sinha, S. (2016). Biological activities of the adenium obesum (forssk.) roem. & schult: A concise review. *Malaya Journal of Biosciences, 2,* 214–21.

Pellegrini, A. D. (2014). Object use in childhood: Development and possible functions. *Behaviour, 150,* 813–43. doi:10.1163/1568539X-00003086.

Pennebaker, J. W. (1997). Writing about emotional experiences as a therapeutic process. *Psychological Science, 8,* 162–66.

Pennebaker, J. W. (2000). The effects of traumatic disclosure on physical and mental health: The values of writing and talking about upsetting events. In J. M. VIolanti, D. Paton, & C. Dunning (Eds.), *Posttraumatic stress intervention: Challenges, issues, and perspectives* (pp. 97–114). Charles C. Thomas.

Pennebaker, J. W., Barger, S. D., & Tiebout, J. (1989). Disclosure of traumas and health of Holocaust survivors. *Psychosomatic Medicine, 51,* 577–89. doi:10.1097/00006842–198909000–00009.

Pennebaker, J. W., & Beall, S. K. (1986). Confronting a traumatic event: Toward an understanding of inhibition and disease. *Journal of Abnormal Psychology, 95,* 274–81. doi:10.1037/0021-843X.95.3.274.

Pennebaker, J. W., & Chung, C. K. (2012). Expressive writing and its links to mental and physical health. In H. S. Friedman (Ed.), *Oxford handbook of health psychology* (pp. 417–37). Oxford University Press. doi:10.1093/oxfordhb/ 9780195342819.013.0018.

Pentiuc, E. J. (2014). *The old testament in eastern orthodox tradition.* Oxford Scholarship Online. doi:10.1093/acprof:oso/9780195331226.001.0001.

Peterson, C., Park, N., Pole, N., D'Andrea, W., & Seligman, M. E. (2009). Strengths of character and posttraumatic growth. *Journal of Traumatic Stress, 21,* 214–17. doi:10.1002/jts.20332.

Piaget, J. (1954). *Play, dreams and imitation in childhood.* Norton.

Porges, S. W. (2011). *The polyvagal theory: Neurophysiological foundations of emotion, communication, attachment, communication and self-regulation.* Norton.

Prati, G., & Pietrantoni, L. (2009). Optimism, social support, and coping strategies as factors contributing to posttruamatic growth: A meta-analysis. *Journal of Loss and Trauma, 14,* 364–88. doi:10.1080/15325020902724271.

Price, C. S. (2008). *The real faith.* Enloe Ministries Publications.

Rankin, A. B., & Taucher, L. C. (2011). A task-oriented approach to art therapy in trauma treatment. *Journal of the American Art Therapy Association, 20,* 138–47. doi:10.1080 /07421656.2003.10129570.

Rhodes, A. M. (2015). Claiming peaceful embodiment through yoga in the aftermath of trauma. *Complementary Therapies in Clinical Practice, 21,* 247–56. doi:10.1016/j. ctcp.2015.09.004.

Rodriquez-Rey, R., Palacios, A., Alonso-Tapia, J., Pérez, J., Alvarez, E., Coca, A., Mencía, S., Marcos, A. M., Mayordomo-Colunga, J., Fernández, F., Gómez, F., Cruz, J., Barón, L., Calderón, R. M., & Belda, S. (2016). Posttraumatic growth in pediatric intensive care personnel: Dependence on resilience and coping strategies. *Psychological Trauma: Theory, Research, Practice, and Policy,* 1–9. doi:10.1037/tra0000211.

Rohr, R. (2003). *Everything belongs: The gift of contemplative prayer.* Crossroad.

Rohr, R. (2008). *Things hidden: Scripture as spirituality.* Franciscan Media.

Rohr, R. (2009). *The naked now: Learning to see as the mystics see.* Crossroad.

Rohr, R. (2011). *Wondrous encounters: Scriptures for Lent.* Saint Anthony Messenger Press.

Rohr, R. (2014). *Eager to love: The alternative way of St. Francis.* Franciscan Media.

Rothenberg, A. (2015). *Flight from wonder: A scientific investigation of creativity.* Oxford University Press.

Runco, M. A. (2004). Everyone has creative potential. In R. J. Sternberg, E. L. Grigorenko, & J. L. Singer (Eds.), *Creativity: From potential to realization* (pp. 21–30). American Psychological Association.

Russ, S. W. (1993). *Affect and creativity: The role of affect and play in the creative process.* Erlbaum.

Russ, S. W. (2004). *Play in child development and psychotherapy: Toward empirically supported practice.* Erlbaum.

Russ, S. W. (2014). *Pretend play in childhood: Foundation of adult creativity.* American Psychological Association.

Russ, S. W., & Wallace, C. E. (2013). Pretend play and creative processes. *The American Journal of Play, 6,* 136–48.

Rytwinski N. K., Scur, M. D., Feeny, N. C., & Youngstrom, E. A. (2013). The co-occurrence of major depressive disorder among individuals with posttraumatic stress disorder: A meta-analysis. *Journal of Traumatic Stress, 26*(3), 299–309. doi:10.1002/jts.21814.

Sandelands, L. E. (2013). The romance of wonder in organization studies. *Journal of Management, Spirituality and Religion, 10,* 358–79. doi:10.1080/14766086.2013.80 1024.

Sarna, N. M. (1989). *Genesis commentary.* Jewish Publication Society.

Saul, J. (2013). *Collective trauma, collective healing: Promoting community resilience in the aftermath of disaster.* Routledge.

Sawyer, R. K. (2006). *Explaining creativity: The science of human innovation.* Oxford University Press.

Schore, A. N. (2001). The seventh annual John Bowlby memorial lecture, minds in the making: Attachment, the self-organizing brain, and developmentally oriented psychoanalytic psychotherapy. *British Journal of Psychother*apy, *17,* 299–328.

Schore, A. N. (2003). *Affect regulation and the repair of the self.* Norton.

Schore, A. N. (2011). *The science of the art of psychotherapy.* Norton.

Sears, S. Stanton, A. L., & Danoff-Burg, S. (2003). The yellow brick road and the emerald city: Benefit finding, positive reappraisal coping, and posttraumatic growth in women with early-stage breast cancer. *Health Psychology, 22,* 487–97. doi:10.1037/0278–6133.22.5.487.

Shapleske, J., Rossell, S. L. Woodruff, P. W. R., & David, A. S. (1999). The planum temporale: A systematic, quantitative review of its structural, functional and clinical significance. *Brain Research Reviews, 29,* 26–49.

Shaw, M. P., & Runco, M. A. (1994). Conclusions concerning creativity and affect. In M. P. Shaw & M. A. Runco (Eds.), *Creativity research: Creativity and affect* (pp. 261–70). Ablex Publishing.

Shults, F. L., & Sandage, S. J. (2006). *Transforming spirituality: Integrating theology and psychology.* Baker Academic.

Siegel, D. J. (1999). *The developing mind: How relationships and the brain interact to shape who we are.* Guilford.

Simon, J. (2013). *Adenium Obesum.* Flickr. https://flic.kr/p/fQfYjJ.

Simpson, S. W. (2014). *Discussion of Tolkien reader, clinical interventions: Psychodynamic, week 9* [Lecture]. Fuller Theological Seminary, Pasadena, California.

Smith, J. B. (2017). *The magnificent story: Uncovering a gospel of goodness, beauty, and truth*. InterVarsity Press.

Stanton, A. L., & Low, C. A. (2004). Toward understanding post traumatic growth: Commentary on Tedeschi and Calhoun. *Psychological Inquiry, 15,* 76–80.

Steger, M. F., & Park, C. L. (2012). The creation of meaning following trauma: Meaning making and trajectories of distress and recovery. In R. A. MckMackin, E. Newman, J. M. Fogler, & T. M. Keane (Eds.), *Trauma therapy in context: The science and craft of evidence-based practice* (pp. 171–91). doi:10.1037/13746–008.

Stellar, J. E., Gordon, A., Anderson, C. L., Piff, P. K., McNeil, G. D., & Keltner, D. (2017). Awe and humility. *Journal of Personality and Social Psychology.* Advance online publication. doi:10.1037.pspi0000109.

Sternberg, R. J. (1985). Implicit theories of intelligence, creativity, and wisdom. *Journal of Personality and Social Psychology, 49,* 607–27.

Sternberg, R. J. (2003). *Wisdom, intelligence, and creativity synthesized.* Cambridge University Press.

Stockton, H., Joseph, S., & Hunt, N. (2014). Expressive writing and posttraumatic growth: An internet-based study. *Traumatology: An International Journal, 20,* 75–83. doi:10/1037/h0099377.

Strickland, B. R. (1989). Internal/external control expectancies: From contingency to creativity. *American Psychologist, 44,* 112.

Strong, J. (2003). *New Strong's exhaustive concordance.* Thomas Nelson.

Sumsion, H., & Alexander, C. F. (1985). *Praise to the lord of our salvation: St. Patrick's breastplate: Anthem for SATB and organ.* Oecumuse.

Tedeschi, R. G., & Calhoun, L. G. (1995). *Trauma and transformation.* Sage.

Tedeschi, R. G., & Calhoun, L. G. (1998). Posttraumatic growth: Future directions. In L. G. Calhoun & R. G. Tedeschi (Eds.), *Posttraumatic growth: Positive changes in the aftermath of crisis* (pp. 215–38). Erlbaum.

Tedeschi, R. G., & Kilmer, R. P. (2005). Assessing strengths, resilience, and growth to guide clinical interventions. *Professional Psychology: Research and Practice, 36,* 230–37. http://dx.doi.org/10.1037/0735-7035-7028.36.3.230.

Tedeschi, R. G., Shakespeare-Finch, J., Taku, K., & Calhoun, L. G. (2018). *Posttraumatic growth: Theory, research and applications.* Routledge.

Thege, B. K., Horwood, L., Slater, L., Tan, M. C., Hodgins, D. C., & Wild, T. C. (2017). Relationship between interpersonal traumatic exposure and addictive behaviors: A systematic review. *BMC Psychiatry, 17,* 164. doi:10.1186/s12888–017–1323–1.

Thurman, H. (1949). *Jesus and the disinherited.* Abingdon.

Tolkien, J. R. R. (1954). *The lord of the rings.* Houghton-Mifflin Harcourt.

Tolkien, J. R. R. (1966). *The Tolkien reader.* Ballantine.

Tolkien, S. (2017, January 3). *Tolkien's grandson on how WW1 inspired lord of the rings.* BBC. http://www.bbc.com/culture/story/20161223-tolkiens-grandson-on-how-ww1-inspired-the-lord-of-the-rings.

Torrance, E. P. (1965). Scientific views of creativity and factors affecting its growth. *Daedalus, 94,* 663–81.

Torrance, E. P. (1993). Understanding creativity: Where to start? *Psychological Inquiry, 4,* 232–34. doi:10.1207/s15327965pli0403_17.

Tortora, S. (2014). The importance of being seen: Winnicott, dance movement psychotherapy, and the embodied experience. In M. B. Spelman & T. S. Frances (Eds.), *The Winnicott tradition: Lines of development* (pp. 259–77). Karnac Books.

Trawick-Smith, J. (2014). The physical play and motor development of young children: A review of literature and implications for practice. *The Center for Early Childhood Education, 13,* 1–53.

Triplett, K. N., Tedeschi, R. G., Cann, A., Calhoun, L. G., & Reeve, C. L. (2012). Posttraumatic growth, meaning in life, and life satisfaction in response to trauma. *Psychological Trauma: Theory, Research, Practice, and Policy, 4,* 400–410. doi: 10.1037/a0024204.

Tripp, T. (2016). A body-based bilateral art protocol for reprocessing trauma. In J. L. King (Ed.), *Art therapy, trauma and neuroscience: Theoretical and practical perspectives* (pp. 173–94). Routledge.

Ulanov, A. B. (2005). *Finding space: Winnicott, god, and psychic reality.* Westminster John Knox.

United Methodist Church. (2019). *What is a Tenebrae service?* UMC. http://www.umc.org/what-we-believe/what-is-a-tenebrae-service.

Van der Kolk, B. (2003). Posttraumatic stress disorder and the nature of trauma. In M. F. Solomon and D. J. Siegel (Eds.), *Healing trauma: Attachment, mind, body and brain* (pp. 168–95). Norton.

Van der Kolk, B. (2014). *The body keeps the score: Brain, mind, and body in the healing of trauma.* Penguin.

Veiselmeyer, J., Holguin, J., & Mezulis, A. (2016). The role of resilience and gratitude in posttraumatic stress and post traumatic growth following a campus shooting. *Psychological Trauma: Theory, Research, Practice and Policy, 9,* 1–8. doi:10.1037/tra0000149.

Waddington, R. (2015). *Adenium Obesum, sth, Ethiopia.* Flickr. https://flic.kr/p/2juvo1S.

Waddington, R. (2015). *Desert Rose, Omo, Ethiopia.* Flickr. https://flic.kr/p/rG3rCb.

Waddington, R. (2019). *Adenium Obesum – socotram bottle tree.* Flickr. https://flic.kr/p/2hXkGWR.

Wanklyn, S. G., Pukay-Martin, N. D., Belus, J. M., Cyr, K. S., Girard, T. A., & Monson, C. M. (2016). Trauma types as differential predictors of posttraumatic stress disorder (PTSD), major depressive disorder (MDD), and their comorbidity. *Canadian Journal of Behavioural Science, 48,* 296–305. doi:10.1037/cbs0000056.

Watson, R. A. (2001). Toward union in love: The contemplative spiritual tradition and contemporary psychoanalytic theory in the formation of persons. In T. W. Hall & M. R. McMinn (Eds.), *Spiritual formation, counseling, and psychotherapy* (pp. 53–69). Nova Science Publishers.

Wild, N. D., & Paivo, S. C. (2016). Psychological adjustment, coping, and emotional regulation as predictors of post traumatic growth. *Journal of Aggression, Maltreatment and Trauma, 8,* 97–122. doi:10.1300/J146v08n04_05.

Winnicott, D. W. (1953). Transition objects and transitional phenomena: A study of the first not-me possession. *International Journal of Psychoanalysis, 34,* 89–97.

Winnicott, D. W. (1954). Mind and its relation to the psyche-soma. *British Journal of Medical Psychology, 27*(4), 201–9. doi:10.1111/j.2044-8341.1954.tb00864.x.

Winnicott, D. W. (1964). Review of memories, dreams and reflections. In C. Winnicott, R. Shepherd, & M. Davis (Eds.), *Psychoanalytic explorations* (pp. 482–92). Harvard University Press.

Winnicott, D. W. (1965). *The maturational processes and the facilitating environment: Studies in the theory of emotional development.* International Universities Press.

Winnicott, D. W. (1971). *Playing and reality.* Routledge.

Wright, N. T. (2006). *The road to new creation.* N. T. Wright Page. http://ntwrightpage.com/2016/03/30/the-road-to-new-creation/.

Xu, J., & Liao, Q. (2011). Prevalence and predictors of posttraumatic growth among adult survivors one year following 2008 Sichuan earthquake. *Journal of Affective Disorders, 133,* 274–80. doi:10.101 6/j.jad.2011.03.034.

Yarvis, J. S., & Schiess, L. (2009). Subthreshold posttraumatic stress disorder (PTSD) as a predictor of depression, alcohol use, and health problems in veterans. *Journal of Workplace Behavioural Health, 4,* 395–424.

Yong, A. (2010). *Who is the holy spirit?* Paraclete.

Zaidi, L. Y., & Foy, D. W. (1994). Childhood abuse experiences and combat-related PTSD. *Journal of Traumatic Stress, 7,* 33–42. http://dx.doi.org/10.1002/jts.2490070105.

Index